The Mystic Will

A Method of Developing and Strengthening the Faculties of the Mind, through the Awakened Will, by a Simple, Scientific Process Possible to Any Person of Ordinary Intelligence

Charles Godfrey Leland

years much more valuable that all that *a priori* philosophy or psychology ever yielded since the beginning. And, finally, that the leading faculties or powers of the mind, such as Will, Memory, the Constructive faculty, and all which are subject to them, instead of being entirely mysterious "gifts," or inspirations bestowed on only a very few to any liberal extent, are in all, and may be developed grandly and richly by direct methods which are moreover extremely easy, and which are in accordance with the spirit of the age, being the legitimate results of Evolution and Science.

And, that I may not be misunderstood, I would say that the doctrine of Duty agrees perfectly with every form of religion—a man may be Roman Catholic, Church of England, Presbyterian, Agnostic, or what he will; and, if a form aids him in the least to be *sincerely honest*, it would be a pity for him to be without it. Truly there are degrees in forms, and where I live in Italy I am sorry to see so many abuses or errors in them. But to know and do what is right, when understood, is recognising God as nearly as man can know him, and to do this perfectly we require *Will*. It is the true *Logos*.

CHAPTER I.

ATTENTION AND INTEREST.

> "To the fairies, Determination and Good-Will, all things are possible."—*TheManoftheFamily* ,by C. REID.

It happened recently to me, as I write, to see one afternoon lying on the side walk in the Via Calzaioli in Florence what I thought was a common iron screw, about three inches in length, which looked as if it had been dropped by some workman. And recalling the superstition that it is lucky to find such an object, or a nail, I picked it up, when to my astonishment I found that it was a silver pencil case, but made to exactly resemble a screw. Hundreds of people had, perhaps, seen it, thought they knew all about it, or what it was, and then passed it by, little suspecting its real value.

There is an exact spiritual parallel for this incident or parable of the screw-pencil in innumerable ideas, at which well-nigh everybody in the hurrying stream of life has glanced, yet no one has ever examined, until someone with a poetic spirit of curiosity, or inspired by quaint superstition, pauses, picks one up, looks into it, and finds that It has ingenious use, and is far more than it appeared to be. Thus, if I declare that by special attention to a subject, earnestly turning it over and thinking deeply into it, very remarkable results may be produced, as regards result in knowledge, every human being will assent to it as the veriest truism ever uttered; in the fullest belief that he or she assuredly knows all *that*.

Yet it was not until within a very few years that I discovered that this idea, which seemed so commonplace, had within it mysteries and meanings which were stupendously original or remarkable. I found that there was a certain intensity or power of attention, far surpassing ordinary observation, which we may, if we will, summon up and *force* on ourselves, just as we can by special effort see or hear far better at times than usually. The Romans show by such a phrase as *animumadjicer e*, and numerous proverbs and synonyms, that they had learned to bend their attention energetically. They were good listeners, therefore keen observers.

Learning to control or strengthen the Will is closely allied to developing Attention and Interest, and for reasons which will soon be apparent, I will first consider the latter, since they constitute a preparation or basis for the former. And as preliminary, I will consider the popular or common error to the effect that everyone has alloted to him or to her just so much of the faculty of attention or interest as it has pleased Nature to give—the same being true as regards Memory, Will, the Constructive or Artistic abilities, and so on—when in very truth and on the warrant of Experience all may be increased *ad infinitum.* Therefore, we find ignorant men complacently explaining their indifference to art and literature or culture on the ground that they take no interest in such subjects, as if interest were a special heaven-sent gift. Who has not heard the remark, "He or she takes such an *interest* in so many things—I wish that I could." Or, as I heard it very recently expressed, "It must be delightful to be able to interest one's self in something at any time." Which was much the same as the expression of the Pennsylvania German girl, *"AchGott!* I wisht I hat genius und could make a pudden!"

No one can be expected to take an interest at once and by mere will in any subject, but where an earnest and serious Attention has been directed to it, Interest soon follows. Hence it comes that those who deliberately train themselves in Society after the precept enforced by all great writers of social maxims to listen politely and patiently, are invariably rewarded by acquiring at last shrewd intelligence, as is well known to diplomatists. That mere stolid patience subdues impatience sounds like a dull common-place saying, but it is a silver pencil disguised as an iron screw; there is a deep subtlety hidden in it, if it be allowed with a little intelligence, *forethought*, and determination towards a purpose. Let us now consider the mechanical and easy processes by which attention may be awakened.

According to ED. VON HARTMANN, Attention is either spontaneous or reflex. The voluntary fixing our mind upon, or choosing an idea, image, or subject, is *spontaneous attention,* but when the idea for some reason impresses itself upon us then we have enforced, or *reflex attention.* That is simply to say, there is active or passive observation—the things which we seek or which come to us unsought. And the "seeking for," or spontaneous action can be materially aided and made persevering, if before we begin the search or set about devoting Attention to anything, we pause, as it were, to determine or resolve that we *will* be thorough, and not leave off until we shall have mastered it. For strange as it may seem, the doing this actually has in most cases a positive, and very often a remarkable result, as the reader may very easily verify for himself. This Forethought is far more easily awakened, or exerted, than Attention itself, but it prepares it, just as Attention prepares Interest.

Attention is closely allied to Memory; when we would give attention to a subject for continued consideration, we must "memorize" it, or it will vanish. Involuntary memory excited by different causes often compels us to attend to many subjects whether we will or not. Everyone has been haunted with images or ideas even unto being tormented by them; there are many instances in which the Imagination has given them objective form, and they have appeared visibly to the patient. These haunting ideas, disagreeable repetitions or obstinate continuances, assume an incredible variety of forms, and enter in many strange ways into life. Monomania or the being possessed with one idea to the exclusion of others, is a form of overstrained attention, sustained by memory. It is *enforced*.

Mere repetition of anything to almost anybody, will produce remarkable results; or a kind of Hypnotism Causing the patient to yield to what becomes an irresistible power. Thus it is said that perpetual dropping will wear away stones. Dr. JAMES R. COCKE in his "Hypnotism," in illustrating this, speaks of a man who did not want to sign a note, he knew that it was folly to do so, but yielded from having been "over persuaded." I have read a story in which a man was thus simply *talked* into sacrificing his property. The great power latent in this form of suggestiveness is well known to knaves in America where it is most employed. This is the whole secret of the value of advertising. People yield to the mere repetition in time. Attention and Interest may in this way be self-induced from repetition.

It is true that an image or idea may be often repeated to minds which do not think or reflect, without awakening attention; *percontra,* the least degree of thought in a vast majority of cases forms a nucleus, or beginning, which may easily be increased to an indefinite extent. A very little exercise of the Will suffices in most cases to fix the attention on a subject, and how this can be done will be shown in another chapter. But in many cases Attention is attracted with little or no voluntary effort. On this fact is based the truth that when or where it is desired, Attention and Interest may be awakened with great ease by a simple process.

It may be remarked on the subject of repetition of images or ideas, that a vast proportion of senseless superstitions, traditions or customs, which no one can explain, originate in this way, and that in fact what we call *habit* (which ranks as second nature) is only another form or result of involuntary attention and the unconsciously giving a place in the memory to what we have heard.

From the simple fact that even a man of plain common-sense and strong will may be driven to sleeplessness, or well nigh to madness, by the haunting presence of some wretched trifle, some mere jingle or rhyme, or idle memory, we may infer that we have here a great power which *must* in some way be capable of being led to great or useful results by some very easy process. I once wrote a sketch, never completed, in which I depicted a man of culture who, having lost an old manuscript book which he had regarded in a light, semi-incredulous manner as a *fetish,* or amulet, on which his luck depended, began to be seriously concerned, and awaking to the fact, deliberately cultivated his alarm as a psychological study, till he found himself, even with his eyes wide open as an observer in terrible fear, or a semi-monomaniac. The recovery of his lost charm at once relieved him. This was a diversion of Attention for a deliberate purpose, which might have been varied *ad infinitum* to procure very useful results. But I have myself known a man in the United States, who, having lost—he being an actor or performer—a certain article of theatrical properties on which he believed "luck" depended, lost all heart and hope, and fell into a decline, from which he never recovered. In this, as in all such cases, it was not so much conviction or reason which influenced the sufferer as the mere effect of Attention often awakened till it had become what is known as a fixed idea.

A deliberate reflection on what I have here advanced can hardly fail to make it clear to any reader that if he really desires to take an interest in any subject, it is possible to do so, because Nature has placed in every mind vast capacity for attention or fixing ideas, and where the Attention is fixed, Interest, by equally easy process, may always be induced to follow. And note that these preliminary preparations should invariably be as elementary and easy as possible, this being a condition which it is impossible to exaggerate. In a vast majority of cases people who would fain be known as taking an interest in Art begin at the wrong end, or in the most difficult manner possible, by running through galleries where they only acquire a superficial knowledge of results, and learn at best how to *talk* showily about what they have skimmed. Now to this end a good article in a cyclopædia, or a small treatise like that of TAINE'S "Æsthetic" thoroughly read and re-read, till it be really mastered, and then verified by study of a very few good pictures in a single collection, will do more to awaken sincere *interest* than the loose ranging through all the exhibitions in the world. I have read in many novels thrilling descriptions of the effect and results when all the glories of the Louvre or Vatican first burst upon some impassioned and unsophisticated youth, who from that moment found himself an Artist—but I still maintain that it would have been a hundred times better for him had his Attention and Interest been previously attracted to a few pictures, and his mind accustomed to reflect on them.

Be the subject in which we would take an interest artistic or scientific, literary or social, the best way to begin herewith is to carefully read the simplest and easiest account of it which we can obtain, in order that we may know just exactly what it is, or its definition. And this done, let the student at once, while the memory is fresh in mind, follow it up by other research or reading, observations or inquiries, on the same subject, for three books read together on anything will profit more than a hundred at long intervals. In fact, a great deal of broken, irregular or disjointed reading is often as much worse than none at all, as a little coherent study is advantageous.

Many people would very willingly take an interest in many subjects if they knew how. It is a melancholy thing to see a man retired from business with literally nothing to do but fritter away his time on nothings when he might be employed at something absorbing and useful. But they hesitate to *act* because, as is the rule in life, they see everything from its most difficult and repulsive side. There is no man who could not easily take an intelligent interest in Art in some form, but I venture to say that a majority of even educated people who had never taken up the subject would be appalled at it in their secret hearts, or distrust its "use" or their own capacity to master it. Or again, many put no faith in easy manuals to begin with, believing, in their ignorance, that a mere collection of rudiments cannot have much in it. We are all surrounded by thousands of subjects in which we might all take an interest, and do good work, if we would, selecting one, give it a little attention, and by easy process proceed to learn it. As it is, in general society the man or woman who has any special pursuit, accomplishment, or real interest for leisure hours, beyond idle gossip and empty time-killing, is a great exception. And yet I sincerely believe that in perhaps a majority of cases there is a sincere desire to do something, which is killed by simple ignorance of the fact that with a very little trouble indeed interest in something is within the easy reach of all.

I have dwelt on this subject that the reader may be induced to reflect on the fact, firstly, that if he wishes to learn how to develop his Will and strengthen it, it is absolutely necessary to take an *interest* in it. I beg him to consider how this art of acquiring attention and interest has been, or is, obscured in most minds, and the difficulties of acquiring it, exaggerated. Secondly, I would point out that the method of process for making a Will is so closely allied to that laid down for Attention that it will seem like a deduction from it, both being allied to what may claim to be an original Art of Memory, to which I shall devote a chapter in its due place.

For as I hope clearly to prove it is an easy matter to create a strong will, or strengthen that which we have, to a marvelous extent, yet he who would do this must first give his *Attention* firmly and fixedly to his intent or want, for which purpose it is absolutely necessary that he shall first *know his own mind regarding what he means to do,* and therefore meditate upon it, not dreamily, or vaguely, but earnestly. And this done he must assure himself that he takes a real interest in the subject, since if such be the case I may declare that his success is well nigh certain.

And here it may be observed that if beginners, *before* taking up any pursuit, would calmly and deliberately consider the virtues of Attention and Interest, and how to acquire them, or bring them to bear on the proposed study or work, we should hear much less of those who had "begun German" without learning it, or who failed in any other attempt. For there would in very truth be few failures in life if those who undertake anything first gave to it long and careful consideration by leading observation into every detail, and, in fact, becoming familiar with the idea, and not trusting to acquire interest and perseverance in the future. Nine-tenths of the difficulty and doubt or ill-at-easeness which beginners experience, giving them the frightened feeling of "a cat in a strange garret," and which often inspires them to retreat, is due entirely to not having begun by training the Attention or awakened an Interest in the subject.

It has often seemed to me that the reason for failure, or the ultimate failing to attain success, in a vast number of "Faith cures," is simply because the people who seek them, being generally of a gushing, imaginative nature, are lacking in deep reflection, application, or earnest attention. They are quick to take hold, and as quick to let go. Therefore, they are of all others the least likely to seriously reflect *beforehand* on the necessity of preparing the mind to patience and application. Now it seems a simple thing to say, and it is therefore all the harder to understand, that before going to work at anything which will require perseverance and repeated effort we can facilitate the result amazingly by thinking over and anticipating it, so that when the weariness comes it will not be as a discouraging novelty, but as something of course, even as a fisherman accepts his wet feet, or the mosquitoes. But how this disposition to grow weary of work or to become inattentive may be literally and very completely conjured away will be more fully explained in another chapter. For this let it suffice to say that earnest *forethought,* and the more of it the better, bestowed on aught which we intend to undertake, is a thing rarely attempted in the real sense in which I mean it, but which, when given, eases every burden and lightens every toil.

Mere *forethought* repeated is the easiest of mental efforts. Yet even a little of it asserted before undertaking a task will wonderfully facilitate the work.

"Hypnotism," says Dr. JAMES R. COCKE, "can be used to train the attention of persons habitually inattentive." But, in fact, forethinking in any way is the minor or initiatory stage of Suggestion. Both are gradual persuasion of the nervous system into habit.

And on this text a marvelous sermon could be preached, which, if understood, would sink deeply into every heart, inspiring some while alarming others, but greatly cheering the brave. And it is this. There are millions of people who suffer from irritability, want of self-control, loquacity, evil in many forms, or nerves, who would fain control themselves and stop it all. Moralists think that for this it is enough to convince their reason. But this rarely avails. A man may *know* that he is wrong, yet *not* be able to reform. Now, what he wants is to have his attention fixed long enough to form a new habit. Find out how this can be done, and it may in many cases be the simplest and most mechanical thing in the world to cure him. Men have been frightened by a scarecrow into thorough repentance. "A question of a few vibrations of ether, more or less, makes for us all the difference between perception and non-perception," or between sight and blindness. Accustom any such moral invalid to being Suggested or willed a few times into a calm, self-controlled state and the habit may be formed.

And to those who doubt, and perhaps would sneer, I have only to say *try it.* It will do them good.

CHAPTER II.

SELF-SUGGESTION.

> "In thy soul, as in a sleep,
> Gods or fiends are hidden deep,
> Awful forms of mystery,
> And spirits, all unknown to thee:
> Guard with prayer, and heed with care,
> Ere thou wak'st them from their lair!"

The records of the human race, however written, show that Man has always regarded himself as possessed of latent faculties, or capacities of a mysterious or extraordinary nature: that is to say, transcending in scope or power anything within the range of ordinary conscious mental capacity. Such for example is the Dream, in which there occurs such a mingling of madness with mysterious intuitions or memories that it is no wonder it has always been regarded as allied to supernatural intelligence. And almost as general as the faith in dreams as being *weird* (in the true sense of the much-abused word) or "strangely prophetic," is that in *fascination*, or that one human being can exercise over another by a mystic will and power a strong influence, even to the making the patient do whatever the actor or superior requires.

However interesting it may be, it is quite needless for the purpose which I have in view to sketch the history of occultism, magic or sorcery from the earliest times to the present day. Fascination was, however, its principal power, and this was closely allied to, or the parent of, what is now known as Suggestion in Hypnotism. But ancient magic in its later days certainly became very much mixed with magnetism in many phases, and it is as an off-shoot of Animal Magnetism that Hypnotism is now regarded, which is to be regretted, since it is in reality radically different from it, as several of the later writers of the subject are beginning to protest. The definition and differences of the two are as follows: Animal Magnetism, first formulized by ANTON MESMER from a mass of more or less confused observations by earlier writers, was the doctrine that there is a magnetic fluid circulating in all created forms, capable of flux and reflux, which is specially active or potent in the human body. Its action may be concentrated or increased by the human will, so as to work wonders, one of which is to cause a person who is magnetized by another to obey the operator, this obedience being manifested in many very strange ways.

Still there were thousands of physiologists or men of science who doubted the theory of the action or existence of Animal Magnetism, and the vital fluid, as declared by the Mesmerists, and they especially distrusted the marvels narrated of clairvoyance, which was too like the thaumaturgy or wonder-working attributed to the earlier magicians. Finally, the English scientist, BRAID, determined that it was not a magnetic fluid which produced the recognized results, "but that they were of purely subjective origin, depending on the nervous system of the one acted on." That is to say, in ordinary language, it was "all imagination"—but here, as in many other cases, a very comprehensive and apparently common-sensible word is very far from giving an adequate or correct idea of the matter in question—for what the imagination itself really is in this relation is a mystery which is very difficult to solve. I have heard of an old French gentleman who, when in a circus, expressed an opinion that there was nothing remarkable in the wonderful performances of an acrobat on a tight-rope, or trapeze. *"Voyez-vous monsieur"* he exclaimed; *"Ce n'est que la mathématique—rien que ca!"* And only the Imagination—"all your Imagination" is still the universal solvent in Philistia for all such problems.

Hypnotism reduced to its simplest principle is, like the old Fascination, the action of mind upon mind, or of a *mind upon itself,* in such a manner as to produce a definite belief, action, or result. It is generally effected by first causing a sleep, as is done in animal magnetism, during which the subject implicitly obeys the will of the operator, or performs whatever he suggests. Hence arose the term Suggestion, implying that what the patient takes into his head to do, or does, must first be submitted to his own mental action.

Very remarkable results are thus achieved. If the operator, having put a subject to sleep (which he can do in most cases, if he be clever, and the experiments are renewed often enough), will say or suggest to him that on the next day, or the one following, or, in fact, any determined time, he shall visit a certain friend, or dance a jig, or wear a given suit of clothes, or the like, he will, when the hypnotic sleep is over, have forgotten all about it. But when the hour indicated for his call or dance, or change of garment arrives, he will be haunted by such an irresistible feeling that he *must* do it; that in most cases it will infallibly be done. It is no exaggeration to say that this has been experimented on, tested and tried thousands of times with success and incredible ingenuity in all kinds of forms and devices. It would seem as if spontaneous attention went to sleep, but, like an alarm clock, awoke at the fixed hour, and then *reflex* action.

Again—and this constitutes the chief subject of all I here discuss—we can *suggest* to ourselves so as to produce the same results. It seems to be a curious law of Nature that if we put an image or idea into our minds with the preconceived determination or intent that it shall recur or return at a certain time, or in a certain way, after sleeping, it will *do so*. And here I beg the reader to recall what I said regarding the resolving to begin any task, that it can be greatly aided by even a brief pre-determination. In all cases it is a kind of self-suggestion. There would seem to be some magic virtue in sleep, as if it preserved and ripened our wishes, hence the injunction in the proverbs of all languages to sleep over a resolve, or subject—and that "night brings counsel."

It is not necessary that this sleep shall be *hypnotic*, or what is called hypnotic slumber, since, according to very good authorities, there is grave doubt as to whether the so-called condition is a sleep at all. *Hypnotism* is at any rate a suspension of the faculties, resembling sleep, caused by the will and act of the operator. He effects this by fixing the eyes on the patient, making passes as in Mesmerism, giving a glass of water, or simply commanding sleep. And this, as Dr. COCKE has experienced and described, can be produced to a degree by anyone on himself. But as I have verified by experiment, if we, after retiring to rest at night, will calmly yet firmly resolve to do something on the following day, or be as much as possible in a certain state of mind, and if we then fall into ordinary natural sleep, just as usual, we may on waking have forgotten all about it, yet will none the less feel the impulse and carry out the determination.

What gives authority for this assertion, for which I am indebted originally to no suggestion or reading, is the statement found in several authorities that a man can "hypnotize" another without putting him to sleep; that is, make him unconsciously follow suggestion.

I had read in works on hypnotism of an endless number of experiments, how patients were made to believe that they were monkeys or madmen, or umbrellas, or criminals, women or men, *àvolonté,* but in few of them did I find that it had ever occurred to anybody to turn this wonderful power of developing the intellect to any permanent benefit, or to increasing the moral sense. Then it came to my mind since Self-Suggestion was possible that if I would resolve to work *all* the next day; that is, apply myself to literary or artistic labor without once feeling fatigue, and succeed, it would be a marvelous thing for a man of my age. And so it befell that by making an easy beginning I brought it to pass to perfection. What I mean by an easy beginning is not to will or resolve *too* vehemently, but to simply and very gently, yet assiduously, impress the idea on the mind *so as to fall asleep while thinking of it as a thing to be.* My next step was to *will* that I should, all the next day, be free from any nervous or mental worry, or preserve a hopeful, calm, or well-balanced state of mind. This led to many minute and extremely curious experiences and observations. That the imperturbable or calm state of mind promptly set in was undeniable, but it often behaved, like the Angel in H. G. Wells' novel, "The Wonderful Visit," as if somewhat frightened at, or of, with, or by its new abode, and no wonder, for it was indeed a novel guest, and the goblins of "Worry and Tease, Fidget and Fear," who had hitherto been allowed to riot about and come and go at their own sweet mischievous wills, were ill-pleased at being made to keep quiet by this new lady of the manor. And indeed no mere state of mind, however well maintained, can resist everything, and the mildest mannered man may cut a throat under great provocation. I had my lapses, but withal I was simply astonished to find how, by perseverance, habitual calm not only grew on me, but how decidedly it increased. I most assuredly have experienced it to such a degree as to marvel that the method is not more employed as a cure for nervous suffering and insomnia.

But far beyond perseverance in labor, or the inducing a calmer and habitually restful state of mind, was the Awakening of the Will, which I found as interesting as any novel or drama, or series of active adventures which I have ever read or experienced. I can remember when most deeply engaged in it, re-reading DE QUINCEY'S "Confessions of an Opium Eater." I took it by chance on my birthday, August 15, which was also his, and as I read I longed from my very heart that he were alive, that I might consult with him on the marvelous Fairyland which it seemed to me had been discovered—and then I remembered how Dr. TUCKEY, the leading English hypnotist, had once told me how easy it was for his science to completely cure the mania for opium and other vices.

And this is the discovery: Resolve before going to sleep that if there be anything whatever for you to do which requires Will or Resolution, be it to undertake repulsive or hard work or duty, to face a disagreeable person, to fast, or make a speech, to say "No" to anything; in short, to keep up to the mark or make *any* kind of effort that *you* WILL *do it*—as calmly and unthinkingly as may be. Do not desire to do it sternly or forcibly, or in spite of obstacles—but simply and coolly make up your mind to *do it*—and it will much more likely be done. And it is absolutely true—*crede experto*—that if persevered in, this willing yourself to will by easy impulse unto impulse given, will lead to marvelous and most satisfactory results.

There is one thing of which the young or oversanguine or heedless should be warned. Do not expect from self-suggestion, nor anything else in this life, prompt perfection, or the *maximum* of success. You may pre-determine to be cheerful, but if you are very susceptible to bad weather, and the day should be dismal, or you should hear of the death of a friend, or a great disaster of any kind, some depression of spirits *must* ensue. On the other hand, note well that forming habit by frequent repetition of willing yourself to equanimity and cheerfulness, and also to the banishing of repulsive images when they come, will infallibly result in a very much happier state of mind. As soon as you actually begin to realize that you are acquiring such control remember that is the golden hour—and redouble your efforts. *Perseverandovinces.*

I have, I trust, thus far in a few words explained to the reader the *rationale* of a system of mental discipline based on the will, and how by a very easy process the latter may, like Attention and Interest, be gradually awakened.

As I have before declared, everyone would like to have a strong or vigorous will, and there is a library of books or sermons in some form, exhorting the weak to awaken and fortify their wills or characters, but all represent it as a hard and vigorous process, akin to "storm and stress," battle and victory, and none really tell us how to go about it. I have indeed only indicated that it is by self-suggestion that the first steps are taken. Let us now consider the early beginning of the art or science ere discussing further developments.

CHAPTER III.

WILL DEVELOPMENT.

> "Ce domaine de la Suggestion est immense. Il n'y a pas un seul fait de notre vie mentale qui ne puisse être reproduit et exageré artificiellement par ce moyen."—*BinetetFrèr e,Le MagnetismeAnimal.*

Omitting the many vague indications in earlier writers, as well as those drawn from ancient Oriental sources, we may note that POMPONATIUS or POMPONAZZO, an Italian, born in 1462, declared in a work entitled *De naturalium effectuum admirandorum Causis seu de Incantationibus,* that to cure disease it was necessary to use a strong will, and that the patient should have a vigorous imagination and much faith in the *praê cantator.* PARACELSUS asserted the same thing in many passages directly and indirectly. He regarded medicine as magic and the physician as a wizard who should by a powerful will act on the imagination of the patient. But from some familiarity with the works of PARACELSUS—the first folio of the first full edition is before me as I write—I would say that it would be hard to declare what his marvelous mind did *not* anticipate in whatever was allied to medicine and natural philosophy. Thus I have found that long before VAN HELMONT, who has the credit of the discovery, PARACELSUS knew how to prepare silicate of soda, or water-glass.

Hypnotism as practiced at the present day, and with regard to its common results, was familiar to JOHANN JOSEPH GASSNER, a priest in Suabia, of whom LOUIS FIGUIER writes as follows in his *Histoire du Merveilleux danslesT empsModernes,* published in 1860:

"GASSNER, like the Englishman VALENTINE GREAT-RAKES, believed himself called by divine inspiration to cure diseases. According to the precept of proper charity he began at home—that is to say on himself. After being an invalid for five or six years, and consulting, all in vain, many doctors, and taking their remedies all for naught, the idea seized him that such an obstinate malady as his must have some supernatural evil origin, or in other words, that he was possessed by a demon.

"Therefore he conjured this devil of a disorder, in the name of Jesus Christ to leave him—so it left, and the good GASSNER has put it on record that for sixteen years after he enjoyed perfect health and never had occasion for any remedy, spiritual or otherwise.

"This success made him reflect whether all maladies could not be cured by exorcism . . . The experiment which he tried on the invalids of his parish were so successful that his renown soon opened through all Suabia, and the regions roundabout. Then he began to travel, being called for everywhere."

GASSNER was so successful that at Ratisbon he had, it is said, 6,000 patients of all ranks encamped in tents. He cured by simply touching with his hands. But that in which he appears original was that he not only made his patients sleep or become insensible by ordering them to do so but caused them to raise their arms and legs, tremble, feel any kind of pain, as is now done by the hypnotist. "'In a young lady of good family' he caused laughter and weeping, stiffness of the limbs, absence of sight and hearing, and *anæsthesia* so as to make the pulse beat at his will."

M. FIGUIER and others do not seem to have been aware that a century before GASSNER, a PIETRO PIPERNO of Naples published a book in which there was a special exorcism or conjurations, as he calls them, for every known disorder, and that this possibly gave the hint for a system of cure to the Suabian. I have a copy of this work, which is extremely rare, it having been put on the Roman prohibited list, and otherwise suppressed. But GASSNER himself was suppressed ere long, because the Emperor, Joseph II, cloistered—that is to say, imprisoned him for life in the

Monastery of Pondorf, near Ratisbon. One must not be too good or Apostle-like or curative—even in the Church, which discourages *tropdezéle.*

But the general accounts of GASSNER give the impression, which has not been justly conveyed, that he owed his remarkable success in curing himself and others not to any kind of theory nor faith in magnetism, or in religion, so much as unconscious suggestion, aided by a powerful Will which increased with successes. To simply *pray* to be cured of an illness, or even to be cured by prayer, was certainly no novelty to any Catholic or Protestant in those days. The very nature of his experiments in making many people perform the same feats which are now repeated by hypnotizers, and which formed no part of a religious cure, indicate clearly that he was an observer of strange phenomena or a natural philosopher. I have seen myself an Egyptian juggler in Boulak perform many of these as professed *tricks,* and I do not think it was from any imitation of French clairvoyance. He also pretended that it was by an exertion of his Will, aided by magic forms which he read from a book, that he made two boys obey him. It was probably for these tricks which savored of magic that GASSNER was "retired."

Having in the previous pages indicated the general method by which Will may be awakened and strengthened, that the reader may as soon as possible understand the simple principle of action, I will now discuss more fully the important topic of influencing and improving our mental powers by easily induced Attention, or attention guided by simple Foresight, and pre-resolution aided by simple *auto* or self-suggestion. And I believe, with reason, that by these very simple processes (which have not hitherto been tested that I am aware of by any writer in the light in which I view them); the Will, which is the power of all powers and the mainspring of the mind, can be by means of persuasion increased or strengthened *adinfinitum.*

It is evident that GASSNER'S method partakes in equal proportions of the principles of the well-known "*Faith Cure,*" and that of the Will, or of the passive and the active. What is wanting in it is self-knowledge and the very easily awakened *forethought* which, when continued, leads to far greater and much more certain results. Forethought costs little exertion: it is so calmly active that the weakest minds can employ it; but wisely employed it can set tremendous force in action.

As regards GASSNER, it is admissible that many more cures of disease can be effected by what some vaguely call the Imagination, and others Mental Action, than is generally supposed. Science now proves every year, more and more, that diseases are allied, and that they can be reached through the nervous system. In the celebrated correspondence between KANT and HUFELAND there is almost a proof that incipient gout can be cured by will or determination. But if a merely temporary or partial cure can *really* be obtained, or a cessation from suffering, if the ill be really *curable* at all, it is but reasonable to assume that by continuing the remedy or system, the relief will or must correspond to the degree of "faith" in the patient. And this would infallibly be the case if the sufferer *had* the will. But unfortunately the very people who are most frequently relieved are those of the impulsive imaginative kind, who "soon take hold and soon let go," or who are merely attracted by a sense of wonder which soon loses its charm, and so they react.

Therefore if we cannot only awaken the Will, but also keep it alive, it is very possible that we may not only effect great and thorough cures of diseases, but also induce whatever state of mind we please. This may be effected by the action of the minds or wills of others on our own, which influence can be gradually transferred from the operator to the patient himself, as when in teaching a boy to swim the master holds the pupil up until the latter finds that he is unconsciously moving by his own exertion.

What the fickle and "nervous" patients of any kind need is to have the idea kept before their minds continuously. They generally rush into a novelty without Forethought. Therefore they should be trained or urged to forethink or reflect seriously and often on the cure or process proposed. This is the setting of the nail, which is to be driven in by suggestion. The other method is where we act entirely for ourselves both as regards previous preparation and subsequent training.

I here repeat, since the whole object of the book is that certain facts shall be deeply and *clearly* impressed on the reader's mind, that if we *will* that a certain idea shall recur to us on the following, or any other day, and if we bring the mind to bear upon it just before falling asleep, it may be forgotten when we awake, but it will recur to us when the time comes. This is what almost everybody has proved, that if we resolve to awake at a certain hour we generally do so; if not the first time, after a few experiments, *apropos* of which I would remark that "no one should ever expect full success from any first experiment."

Now it is certainly true that we all remember or recall certain things to be done at certain hours, even if we have a hundred other thoughts in the interval. But it would seem as if by some law which we do not understand Sleep or repose acted as a preserver and reviver, nay, as a real strengthener of Thoughts, inspiring them with a new spirit. It would seem, too, as if they came out of Dreamland, as the children in TIECK'S story did out of Fairyland, with new lives. This is, indeed, a beautiful conception, and I may remark that I will in another place comment on the curious fact that we can add to and intensify ideas by thus passing them through our minds in sleep.

Just by the same process as that which enables us to awake at a given hour, and simply by substituting other ideas for that of time, can we acquire the ability to bring upon ourselves pre-determined or desired states of mind. This is Self-Suggestion or deferred determination, be it with or without sleep. It becomes more certain in its result with every new experiment or trial. The great factor in the whole is perseverance or repetition. By faith we can remove mountains, by perseverance we can carry them away, and the two amount to precisely the same thing.

And here be it noted what, I believe, no writer has ever before observed, that as perseverance depends on renewed forethought and reflection, so by continued practice and thought, in self-suggestion, the one practicing begins to find before long that his conscious will is acting more vigorously in his waking hours, and that he can finally dispense with the sleeping process. For, in fact, when we once find that our will is really beginning to obey us, and inspire courage or indifference where we were once timid, there is no end to the confidence and power which may ensue.

Now this is absolutely true. A man may *will* certain things ere he falls asleep. This willing should not be *intense,* as the old animal magnetizers taught; it ought rather to be like a quiet, firm desire or familiarization with what we want, often gently repeated till we fall asleep in it. So the seeker wills or wishes that he shall, during all the next day, feel strong and vigorous, hopeful, energetic, cheerful, bold or calm or peaceful. And the result will be obtained just in proportion to the degree in which the command or desire has impressed the mind, or sunk into it.

But, as I have said: Do not expect that all of this will result from a first trial. It may even be that those who succeed very promptly will be more likely to give out in the end than those who work up from small beginnings. The first step may very well be that of merely selecting some particular object and calmly or gently, yet determinedly directing the mind to it, to be recalled at a certain hoar. Repeat the experiment, if successful add to it something else. Violent effort is un-advisable, yet mere repetition *without thought* is time lost. *Think* while willing what it is you want, *andaboveall,ifyoucan,think withafeelingthattheideaistor   ecurtoyou.*

This acting or working two thoughts at once may be difficult for some readers to understand, though all writers on the brain illustrate it. It may be formulated thus: "I wish to remember tomorrow at four o'clock to visit my bookseller—bookseller's—four o'clock—four o'clock." But with practice the two will become as one conception.

When the object of a state of mind, as, for instance, calmness all day long, is obtained, even partially, the operator (who must, of course, do all to *help himself* to keep calm, should he remember his wish) will begin to believe in himself sincerely, or in the power of his will to compel a certain state of mind. This won, all may be won, by continued reflection and perseverance. It is the great step gained, the alphabet learned, by which the mind may pass to boundless power.

It may be here interesting to consider some of the states of mind into which a person may be brought by hypnotism. When subject to the will of an operator the patient may believe anything—that he is a mouse or a girl, drunk or inspired. The same may result from self-hypnotism by artificial methods which appeal powerfully to the imagination. According to Dr. JAMES R. COCKE many of his patients could induce this by looking at any bright object, a bed of coals, or at smooth running water. It is, of course, to be understood that it is not merely by *looking* that hypnotism is induced. There must be will or determinate thought; but when once brought about it is easily repeated.

"They have the ability," writes Dr. COCKE, "to resist this state or bring it on at will. Many of them describe beautiful scenes from Nature, or some mighty cathedral with its lofty dome, or the faces of imaginary beings." This writer's own first experience of self-hypnotism was very remarkable. He had been told by a hypnotizer to keep the number twenty-six in his mind. He did so, and after hearing a ringing in his ears and then a strange roaring he felt that spirits were all round him—music sounding and a sensation as of expanding.

But self-hypnotizing, by the simple easy process of trusting to ordinary sleep, is better adapted to action delayed, or states of mind. These may be:

A desire to be at peace or perfectly calm. After a few repetitions it will be found that, though irritating accidents may countervene, the mind will recur more and more to calm.

To feel cheerful or merry.

To be in a brave, courageous, hearty or vigorous mood.

To work hard without feeling weary. This I have fully tested with success, and especially mention it for the benefit of students. All of my intimate friends can certify what I here assert.

To keep the faculty of quickness of perception alert, as, for instance, when going out to perceive more than usual in a crowd. A botanist or mineralogist may awaken the faculty with the hope of observing or finding with success.

To be susceptible to beauty, as, for instance, when visiting a scene or gallery. In such cases it means to derive Attention from Will. The habitually trained Forethought or Attention is here a *great* aid to perception.

To read or study keenly and observantly. This is a faculty which can be very much aided by forethought and self-suggestion.

To forgive and forget enemies and injuries. Allied to it is the forgetting and ignoring of all things which annoy, vex, harrass, tease or worry us in any way whatever. To expect perfect immunity in this respect from the unavoidable ills of life is absurd; but having paid great attention to the subject, and experimented largely on it, I cannot resist declaring that it seems to me in very truth that no remedy for earthly suffering was yet discovered equal to this. I generally put the wish into this form: "I will forget and forgive all causes of enmity and anger, and should they arise I determine at once to cast them aside." It is a prayer, as it were, to the Will to stand by me, and truly the will is *Deus in nobis* to those who believe that God helps those who help themselves. For as we can get into the fearful state of constantly recalling all who have ever vexed or wronged us, or nursing the memory of what we hate or despise, until our minds are like sewers or charnel-houses of dead and poisonous things, so we can resolutely banish them, at first by forethought, then by suggestion, and finally by waking will. And verily there are few people living who would not be the better for such exercise. Many there are who say that they would fain forget and be serene, yet cannot. I do not believe this. We can all exorcise our devils—all of them—if we *will*.

To restrain irritability in our intercourse with others. It will not be quite sufficient as regards controlling the temper to merely will, or *wish* to subdue it. We must also will that when the temptation arises it may be preceded by forethought or followed by regret. As it often happens to a young soldier to be frightened or run away the first time he is under fire, and yet learn courage in the future, so the aspirant resolved to master his passions must not doubt because he finds that the first step slips. *Apropos* of which I would note that in all the books on Hypnotism that I have read their authors testify to a certain false quantity or amount of base alloy in the most thoroughly suggested patients. Something of modesty, something of a moral conscience always remains. Thus, as Dr. COCKE declares, Hypnotism has not succeeded in cases suffering from what are called imperative conceptions, or irresistible belief. "Cases suffering from various imperative conceptions are, while possessing their reasons, either irresistibly led by certain impulses or they cannot rid themselves of erroneous ideas concerning themselves and others." This means, in fact, that they had been previously *hypnotised* to a definite conception which had become imperative. As in Witchcraft, it is a law that one sorcerer cannot undo the work of another without extraordinary pains; so in hypnotism it is hard to undo what is already established by a similar agent.

One can will to remember or recall anything forgotten. I will not be responsible that this will invariably succeed at the first time, but that it does often follow continued determination I know from experience. I believe that where an operator hypnotizes a subject it very often succeeds, if we may believe the instances recorded. And I am also inclined to believe that in many cases, though assuredly not in all, whatever is effected by one person upon another can also be brought about in one's self by patience in forethought, self-suggestion, and the continued will which they awaken.

We can revive by this process old well-nigh forgotten trains of thought. This is difficult but possible. It belongs to an advanced stage of experience or may be found in very susceptible subjects. I do not belong at all to the latter, but I have perfectly succeeded in continuing a dream; that is to say, I have woke up three times during a dream, and, being pleased with it, wished it to go on, then fallen asleep and it went on, like three successive chapters in a novel.

We can subdue the habit of worrying ourselves and others needlessly about every trifling or serious cause of irritation which enters our minds. There are many people who from a mere idle habit or self-indulgence and irrepressible loquacity make their own lives and those of others very miserable—as all my readers can confirm from experience. I once knew a man of great fortune, with many depending on him, who vented his ill-temper and petty annoyances on almost everyone to whom he spoke. He was so fully aware of this failing that he at once, in confessing it to a mutual friend, shed tears of regret. Yet he was a millionaire man of business, and had a strong will which might have been directed to a cure. All peevish, fretful and talkative, or even complaining people, should be induced to seriously study this subject.

We can cure ourselves of the habit of profanity or using vulgar language. No one doubts that a negro who believes in sorcery, if told that if he uttered an oath, *Voodoo* would fall upon him and cause him to waste away, would never swear again. Or that a South Sea Islander would not do the same for fear of *taboo*. Now both these forms of sorcery are really hypnotizing by action on belief, and Forethought aided by the sleep process has precisely the same result—it establishes a fixed idea in the mind, or a haunting presence.

We can cure ourselves of intemperance. This was, I believe, first established or extensively experimented on by Dr. CHARLES LLOYD TUCKEY. This can be aided by willing that the liquor, if drunk, shall be nauseating.

We can repress to a remarkable degree the sensations of fatigue, hunger and thirst. Truly no man can defy the laws of nature, but it is very certain that in cases like that of Dr. TANNER, and the Hindu ascetics who were boxed up and buried for many weeks, there must have been mental determination as well as physical endurance. As regards this very important subject of health, or the body, and the degree to which it can be controlled by the mind or will, it is to be observed that of late years physiologists are beginning to observe that all "mental" or corporeal functions are evidently controlled by the same laws or belong to the same organization. If "the emotions, say of anger or love, in their more emphatic forms, are plainly accompanied by varying changes of the heart and blood-vessels, the viscera and muscles," it must follow that changes or excitement in the physical organs must react on the emotions. "All modes of sensibility, whatever their origin," says LUYS, "are physiologically transported into the sensorium. From fiber to fiber, from sensitive element to sensitive element, our whole organism is sensitive; our whole sentient personality, in fact, is conducted just as it exists, into the plexuses of the *sensorium commune*." Therefore, if every sensation in the body acts on the brain by the aid of secondary brains or ganglions, it must be that the brain in turn can in some way act on the body. And this has hitherto been achieved or attempted by magicians, "miracle-mongers," thaumaturgists, mesmerists, and the like, and by the modern hypnotizer, in which we may observe that there has been at every step less and less mysticism or supernaturalism, and a far easier process or way of working. And I believe it may be fairly admitted that in this work I have simplified the process of physically influencing mental action and rendered it easier. The result from the above conclusions being that *we can control many disorders or forms of disease*. This is an immense subject, and it would be impossible within a brief sketch to determine its limits or conditions. That what are called nervous disorders, which are evidently the most nearly allied to emotions—as, for instance, a headache, or other trouble induced by grief—can be removed by joy, or some counteracting emotion or mere faith is very well known and generally believed. But of late science has established that the affinities between the cerebral and other functions are so intimately, extensively and strangely sympathetic or identical that it is becoming impossible to say what disease may not be temporarily alleviated or cured by new discoveries in directing the nervo-mental power or will. The Faith-Cure, Magic, Mesmerism, Religious Thaumaturgy and other systems have given us a vast number of authentic cures of very positive disorders. But from the point of view taken by many people what has been wanting in all is, *firstly,* a clear and simple scientific method free from all spiritualism or wonder, and, *secondly,* the art of *Perfecting the cures by Perseverance.* For what will relieve for an hour can be made to cure forever, if we exercise foresight and make perpetuity a part of our whole plan.

Now, as regards curing disorders, I beg the reader to specially observe that this, like many other works, depends on the state of the mind; nor can it be undertaken with hope of success unless the operator has by previous practice in easy experiments succeeded in perfectly convincing himself that he has acquired control of his will. Thus having succeeded in willing himself to work all day without fatigue, or to pass the day without being irritable, let him begin to consider, reflect and realize that he *can* make himself do this or that, for the more he simply induces the belief and makes himself familiar with it, the stronger and more obedient his Will will be. However, this is simply true that to any self-suggestionist whatever who has had some little practice and attained to even a moderate command over his will, a very great degree of the power to relieve bodily suffering is easy to develop, and it may be increased by practice to an incredible extent. Thus in case of suffering by pain of any kind in another, begin by calmly persuading him or her that relief has been obtained thousands of times by the process, and endeavor to awaken belief, or, at least, so much attention and interest that the fact will remain as *forethought* in the mind. The next step should be to promise relief, and then induce sleep by the showing a coin, passes with the hands, etc., or allowing the subject to sink into a natural slumber. If there be no success the first time, repeat the experiment. Gout, headaches, all forms of positive pain, severe colds, *anæmia, insomnia, melancholia,* and dyspepsia appear to be among the ills which yield most readily to, or are alleviated (to the great assistance of a regular cure), by suggestion.

As regards curing disorders, producing insensibility to hunger and thirst, heat or cold, and the like, all are aware that to a man who is under the influence of some great and overpowering emotion, such as rage or surprise, or joy, no pain is perceptible. In like manner, by means of persuasion, sleep, a temporary oblivion, and the skillfully awakened Will, the same insensibility or ignoring can be effected. There is, however, this to be observed, that while in the vast library of books which teach mental medicine the stress is laid entirely on producing merely a temporary cure I insist that by great Forethought, by conducting the cure with a view to permanence, ever persuading the patient to think on the future, and finally by a very thorough continuation and after-treatment many diseases may be radically removed.

To recapitulate and make all clear we will suppose that the reader desires during the following day to be in a calm, self-possessed or peaceful state of mind. Therefore at night, after retiring, let him first completely consider what he wants and means to acquire. This is the Forethought, and it should be as thorough as possible. Having done this, will or declare that what you want shall come to pass on awaking, and repeating this and thinking on it, fall asleep. This is all. Do not wish for two things at once, or not until your mind shall have become familiar with the process. As you feel your power strengthen with success you may will yourself to do whatever you desire.

CHAPTER IV.

FORETHOUGHT.

"Post fata resurgo."

"What is forethought may sleep—'tis very plain,
But rest assured that it will rise again."

"Forethought is plan inspired by an absolute Will to carry it out."

It may have struck the reader as an almost awful, or as a very wonderful idea, that man has within himself, if he did but know it, tremendous powers or transcendental faculties of which he has really never had any conception. One reason why such bold thought has been subdued is that he has always felt according to tradition, the existence of superior supernatural (and with them patrician) beings, by whose power and patronage he has been effectively restrained or kept under. Hence gloom and pessimism, doubt and despair. It may seem a bold thing to say that it did not occur to any philosopher through the ages that man, resolute and noble and free, might *will* himself into a stage of mind defying devils and phantasms, or that amid the infinite possibilities of human nature there was the faculty of assuming the Indifference habitual to all animals when not alarmed. But he who will consider these studies on Self-Hypnotism may possibly infer from them that we have indeed within us a marvelous power of creating states of mind which make the idea of Pessimism ridiculous. For it renders potent and grand, pleasing or practically useful, to all who practice it, a faculty which has the great advantage that it may enter into all the relations or acts of life; will give to everyone something to do, something to occupy his mind, even in itself, and if we have other occupations, Forethought and Induced Will may be made to increase our interest in them and stimulate our skill. In other words, we can by means of this Art increase our ability to practice all arts, and enhance or stimulate Genius in every way or form, be it practical, musical or plastic.

Since I began this work there fell into my hands an ingenious and curious book, entitled "Happiness as found in *Forethought minus Fearthought*," by HORACE FLETCHER, in which the author very truly declares that *Fear* in some form has become the arch enemy of Man, and through the fears of our progenitors developed by a thousand causes, we have inherited a growing stock of diseases, terrors, apprehensions, pessimisms, and the like, in which he is perfectly right.

But as Mr. FLETCHER declares, if men could take *Forethought* as their principle and guide they would obviate, anticipate or foresee and provide for so many evil contingencies and chances that we might secure even peace and happiness, and then man may become brave and genial, altruistic and earnest, in spite of it all, by *willing* away his Timidity.

I have not assumed a high philosophical or metaphysical position in this work; my efforts have been confined to indicating how by a very simple and well-nigh mechanical process, perfectly intelligible to every human being with an intellect, one may induce certain states of mind and thereby create a Will. But I quite agree with Mr. FLETCHER that Forethought is strong thought, and the point from which all projects must proceed. As I understand it, it is a kind of impulse or projection of will into the coming work. I may here illustrate this with a curious fact in physics. If the reader wished to ring a door-bell so as to produce as much sound as possible he would probably pull it as far back as he could and then let it go. But if he would in letting it go simply give it a tap with his forefinger he would actually redouble the noise.

Or, to shoot an arrow as far as possible, it is not enough to merely draw the bow to its utmost span or tension. If just as it goes you will give the bow a quick *push,* though the effort be trifling, the arrow will fly almost as far again as it would have done without it.

Or, if, as is well known, in wielding a very sharp saber, we make the *draw-cut,* that is if we add to the blow or chop, as with an axe, a certain slight pull and simultaneously, we can cut through a silk handkerchief or a sheep.

Forethought is the tap on the bell, the push of the bow, the draw on the saber. It is the deliberate yet rapid action of the mind when before falling to sleep or dismissing thought we *bid* the mind to subsequently respond. It is more than merely thinking what we are to do; it is the bidding or ordering self to fulfill a task before willing it.

Forethought in the senses employed or implied as here described means much more than mere previous consideration or reflection, which may be very feeble. It is, in fact, "constructive," which, as inventive, implies *active* thought. "Forethought stimulates, aids the success of honest aims." Therefore, as the active principle in mental work, I regard it as a kind of self-impulse, or that minor part in the division of the force employed which sets the major into action. Now, if we really understand this and can succeed in employing Forethought as the preparation for, and impulse to, Self-Suggestion, we shall greatly aid the success of the latter, because the former insures attention and interest. Forethought may be brief, but it should always be energetic. By cultivating it we acquire the enviable talent of those men who take in everything at a glance, and act promptly, like a NAPOLEON. This power is universally believed to be entirely innate or a gift; but it can be induced or developed in all minds in proportion to the will by practice.

Be it observed that as the experimenter progresses in the development of will by suggestion, he can gradually lay aside the latter, or all *processes,* especially if he work to such an end, anticipating it. Then he simply acts by clear will and strength, and Forethought constitutes all his stock-in-trade, process or aid. He preconceives and wills energetically at once, and by practice and repetition *Forethought* becomes a marvelous help on all occasions and emergencies.

To make it of avail the one who frequently practices self-suggestion, at first with, and then without sleep, will inevitably find ere long that to facilitate his work, or to succeed he *must* first write, as it were, or plan a preface, synopsis, or epitome of his proposed work, to start it and combine with it a resolve or decree that it must be done, the latter being the tap on the bell-knob. Now the habit of composing the plan as perfectly, yet as succinctly as possible, daily or nightly, combined with the energetic impulse to send it off, will ere long give the operator a conception of what I mean by Foresight which by description I cannot. And when grown familiar and really mastered its possessor will find that his power to think and act promptly in all the emergencies of life has greatly increased.

Therefore Forethought means a great deal more, as here employed, than seeing in advance, or deliberate prudence—it rather implies, like divination or foreknowledge, sagacity and mental *action* as well as mere perception. It will inevitably or assuredly grow with the practice of self-suggestion if the latter be devoted to mental improvement, but as it grows it will qualify the operator to lay aside the sleep and suggest to himself directly.

All men of great natural strength of mind, gifted with the will to do and dare, the beings of action and genius, act directly, and are like athletes who lift a tree by the simple exertion of the muscles. He who achieves his aim by self-culture, training, or suggestion, is like one who raises the weight by means of a lever, and if he practice it often enough he may in the end become as strong as the other.

There is a curious and very illustrative instance of Forethought in the sense in which I am endeavoring to explain it, given in a novel, the "Scalp-Hunters," by MAYNE REID, with whom I was well acquainted in bygone years. Not having the original, I translate from a French version:

"His aim with the rifle is infallible, and it would seem as if the ball obeyed his Will. There must be a kind of *directing principle* in his mind, independent of strength of nerve and sight. He and one other are the only men in whom I have observed this singular power."

This means simply the exercise in a second, as it were, of "the tap on the bell-knob," or the projection of the will into the proposed shot, and which may be applied to any act. Gymnasts, leapers and the like are all familiar with it. It springs from resolute confidence and self-impulse enforced; but it also creates them, and the growth is very great and rapid when the idea is much kept before the mind. In this latter lies most of the problem.

In Humanity, mind, and especially Forethought, or reflection, combined in one effort with will and energy, enters into all acts, though often unsuspected, for it is a kind of unconscious *reflex* action or cerebration. Thus I once discovered to my astonishment in a gymnasium that the extremely mechanical action of putting up a heavy weight from the ground to the shoulder and from the shoulder to the full reach of the arm above the head, became much easier after a little practice, although my muscles had not grown, nor my strength increased during the time. And I found that whatever the exertion might be there was always some trick or knack, however indescribable, by means of which the man with a brain could surpass a dolt at *anything,* though the latter were his equal in strength. But it sometimes happens that the trick can be taught and even improved on. And it is in all cases Forethought, even in the lifting of weights or the willing on the morrow to write a poem.

For this truly weird power—since "the weird sisters" in "Macbeth" means only the sisters who *foresee*—is, in fact, the energy which projects itself in some manner, which physiology can as yet only very weakly explain, and even if the explanation *were* perfect, it would amount in fact to no more than showing the machinery of a watch, when the main object for us is that it should *keep time,* and tell the hour, as well as exhibit the ingenuity of the maker—which thing is very much lost sight of, even by many very great thinkers, misled by the vanity of showing how much they know.

Yes, Foresight or Forethought projects itself in all things, and it is a serious consideration, or one of such immense value, that when really understood, and above all subjected to some practice—such as I have described, and which, as far as I can see, is *necessary*—one can bring it to bear *intelligently* on all the actions of life, that is to say, to *much* greater advantage than when we use it ignorantly, just as a genius endowed with strength can do far more with it than an ignoramus. For there is nothing requiring Thought in which it cannot aid us. I have alluded to Poetry. Now this does not mean that a man can become a SHAKESPEARE or SHELLEY by means of all the forethought and suggestion in the world, but they will, if well developed and directed, draw out from the mystic depths of mind such talent as he *has*—doubtless in some or all cases more than he has ever shown.

No one can say what is hidden in every memory; it is like the sounding ocean with its buried cities, and treasures and wondrous relics of the olden time. This much we may assume to know, that every image or idea or impression whichever reached us through any of our senses entered a cell when it was ready for it, where it sleeps or wakes, most images being in the former condition. In fact, every brain is like a monastery of the Middle Ages, or a beehive. But it is built on a gigantic scale, for it is thought that no man, however learned or experienced he might be, ever contrived during all his life to so much as even half fill the cells of his memory. And if any reader should be apprehensive lest it come to pass with him in this age of unlimited supply of cheap knowledge that he will fill all his cells let him console himself with the reflection that it is supposed that Nature, in such a case, will have a further supply of new cells ready, she never, as yet, having failed in such rough hospitality, though it often leaves much to be desired!

Yes, they are all there—every image of the past, every face which ever smiled on us—the hopes and fears of bygone years—the rustling of grass and flowers and the roar of the sea—the sound of trumpets in processions grand—the voices of the great and good among mankind—or what you will. Every line ever read in print, every picture and face and house is there. Many an experiment has shown this to be true; also that by mesmerizing or hypnotizing processes the most hidden images or memories can be awakened. In fact, the idea has lost much of its wonder since the time of Coleridge, now that every sound can be recorded, laid away and reproduced, and we are touching closely on an age when all that lies *perdu* in any mind can or will be set forth visibly, and all that a man has ever *seen* be shown to the world. For this is no whit more wonderful than that we can convey images or pictures by telegraph, and when I close my eyes and recall or imagine a form it does not seem strange that there might be some process by means of which it might be photographed.

And here we touch upon the Materialization of Thought, which conception loses a part of the absurdity with which Spiritualists and Occultists have invested it, if we regard all nature as one substance. For, in truth, all that was ever perceived, even to the shadow of a dream by a lunatic, had as real an existence while it lasted as the Pyramids of Egypt, else it could not have been perceived. Sense cannot, even in dreams, observe what is not for the time an effect on matter. If a man *imagines* or makes believe to himself that he has a fairy attendant, or a dog, and *fancies* that he sees it, that man does really see *something,* though it be invisible to others. There is some kind of creative brain-action going on, some employment of atoms and forces, and, if this be so, we may enter it among the Possibilities of the Future that the Material in any form whatever may be advanced, or further materialized or made real.

It is curious that this idea has long been familiar to believers in magic. In more than one Italian legend which I have collected a sorceress or goddess evolves a life from her own soul, as a fire emits a spark. In fact, the fancy occurs in some form in all mythologies, great or small. In one old Irish legend a wizard turns a Thought into a watch-dog. The history of genius and of Invention is that of realizing ideas, of making them clearer and stronger and more comprehensive. Thus it seems to me that the word

Forethought as generally loosely understood, when compared to what it has been shown capable of expressing, is almost as much advanced as if like the fairy HERMELINA, chronicled by GROSIUS, it had been originally a vapor or mere fantasy, and gradually advanced to fairy life so as to become the companion of a wizard.

If an artist, say a painter, will take forethought for a certain picture, whether the subject be determined or not, bringing himself to that state of easy, assured confidence, as a matter of course that he will *retain* the subject he will, if not at the first effort, almost certainly at last find himself possessed of it. Let him beware of haste, or of forcing the work. When he shall have secured suggestive Interest let him will that Ingenuity shall be bolder and his spirit draw from the stores of memory more abundant material. Thus our powers may be gradually and gently drawn into our service. Truly it would seem as if there were *no* limit to what a man can evolve out of himself if he will take Thought thereto.

Forethought can be of vast practical use in cases where confidence is required. Many a young clergyman and lawyer has been literally frightened out of a career, and many an actor ruined for want of a very little knowledge, and in this I speak from personal experience. Let the aspirant who is to appear in public, or pass an examination, and is alarmed, base his forethought on such ideas as this, that he would not be afraid to repeat his speech to *one* person or two—why should he fear a hundred? There are some who can repeat this idea to themselves till it takes hold strongly, and they rise almost feeling contempt for all in court—as did the old lady in Saint Louis, who felt so relieved when a witness at *not* feeling frightened that she bade judge and jury cease looking at her in that impudent way.

Having read the foregoing to a friend he asked me whether I believed that by Forethought and Suggestion a gentleman could be induced without diffidence to offer himself in marriage, since, as is well known, that the most eligible young men often put off wedding for years because they cannot summon up courage to propose. To which I replied that I had no great experience of such cases, but as regarded the method I was like the Scotch clergyman who, being asked by a wealthy man if he thought that the gift of a thousand pounds to the Kirk would save the donor's soul, replied:

"I'm na prepairet to preceesly answer thot question—but I wad vara warmly advise ye to *try* it."

It must be remembered that for the very great majority of cases, if really not for all, the practicer of this process must be of temperate habits, and never attempt after a hearty meal, or drinking freely, to exercise Forethought or Self-Suggestion. Peaceful mental action during sleep requires that there shall be very light labor of digestion, and disturbed or troublesome dreams are utterly incompatible with really successful results. Nor will a single day's temperance suffice. It requires many days to bring the whole frame and constitution into good fit order. Here there can be no evasion, for more than ordinary temperance in food and drink is *absolutely indispensable.*

It is a principle, recognized by all physiologists, that digestion and fixed thought cannot go on together; it is even unadvisable to read while eating. Thus in all the old magical operations, which were, in fact, self-hypnotism, a perfect fast is insisted on with reason. This is all so self-evident that I need not dwell on it. It will be needless for anyone to take up this subject as a trifling pastime, or attempt self-suggestion and development of will with as little earnestness as one would give to a game of cards; for in such a half-way effort time will be lost and nothing come of it. Unless entered on with the most serious resolve to persevere, and make greater effort and more earnestly at every step, it had better be let alone.

All who will persevere with calm determination cannot fail ere long to gain a certain success, and this achieved, the second step is much easier. However, there are many people who after doing all in their power to get to the gold or diamond mines, hasten away even when in the full tide of success, because they are fickle—and it is precisely such people who easily tire who are most easily attracted, be it to mesmerism, hypnotism, or any other wonder. And they are more wearisome and greater foes to true Science than the utterly indifferent or the ignorant.

This work will not have been written in vain should it induce the reader to reflect on what is implied by patient repetition or perseverance, and what an incredible and varied *power* that man acquires who masters it. He who can lead himself, or others, into a *habit* can do anything. Even Religion is, in fact, nothing else. "Religion," said the reviewer of "The Evolution of the

Idea of God," by GRANT ALLEN, "he defines as Custom or Practice—not theory, not theology, not ethics, not spiritual aspirations, but a certain set of more or less similar observances: propitiation, prayer, praise, offerings, the request for Divine favors, the deprecation of Divine anger, or other misfortunes"—in short, Ritual. That is to say, it is the aggregate of the different parts of religion, of which many take one for the whole. But this aggregation was the result of earnest patience and had good results. And it is by the careful analysis and all-round examination of Ideas that we acquire valuable knowledge, and may learn how very few there are current which are more than very superficially understood—as I have shown in what I have said of the Will, the Imagination, Forethought, and many other faculties which are flippantly used to explain a thousand problems by people who can hardly define the things themselves.

CHAPTER V.

WILL AND CHARACTER.

> "And I have felt
> A Presence that disturbs me with the joy
> Of elevated thoughts, a sense sublime
> Of something far more deeply interposed,
> Whose dwelling is . . . all in the mind of man;
> A motion and a spirit that impels
> All thinking things."—*Wordsworth.*

As the vast majority of people are not agreed as to what really constitutes a Gentleman, while a great many seem to be practically, at least, very much abroad as to the nature of a Christian, so it will be found that, in fact, there is a great deal of difference as regards the Will. I have known many men, and some women, to be credited by others, and who very much credited themselves, with having iron wills, when, in fact, their every deed, which was supposed to prove it, was based on brazen want of conscience. Mere want of principle or unscrupulousness passes with many, especially its possessors, for strong *will*. And even decision of character itself, as

MAGINN remarks, is often confounded with talent. "A bold woman always gets the name of clever"—among fools—"though her intellect may be of a humble order, and her knowledge contemptible." Among the vulgar, especially those of greedy, griping race and blood, the children of the thief, a robber of the widow and orphan, the scamp of the syndicate, and soulless "promoter" in South or North America, bold robbery, or Selfishness without scruple or timidity always appears as Will. But it is not the whole of the real thing, or real will in itself. When MUTIUS CAIUS SCAEVOLA thrust his hand into the flames no one would have greatly admired his endurance if it had been found that the hand was naturally insensible and felt no pain. Nor would there have been any plaudits for MARCUS CURTIUS when he leapt into the gulf, had he been so drunk as not to know what he was about. The will which depends on unscrupulousness is like the benumbed hand or intoxicated soul. Quench conscience, as a sense of right and obligation, and you can, of course, do a great deal from which another would shrink—and therefore be called "weak-minded" by the fools.

There is another type of person who imposes on the world and on self as being strong-minded and gifted with Will. It is the imperturbable cool being, always self-possessed, with little sympathy for emotion. In most cases such minds result from artificial training, and they break down in real trials. I do not say that they cannot weather a storm or a duel, or stand fire, or get through what novelists regard as superlative stage trials; but, in a moral crisis, the gentleman or lady whose face is all Corinthian brass is apt like that brass in a fire to turn pale. These folk get an immense amount of undeserved admiration as having Will or self-command, when they owe what staying quality they have (like the preceding class) rather to a lack of good qualities than their inspiration.

There are, alas! not a few who regard *Will* as simply identical with mere obstinacy, or stubbornness, the immovability of the Ass, or Bull, or Bear—that is, they reduce it to an animal power. But, as this often or generally amounts in animal or man to mere insensible sulkiness—as far remote as possible from enlightened mental action, it is surely unjust to couple it with the *Voluntary* or pure intelligent *Will*, by which all must understand the very acme of active Intellect.

Therefore it follows, that the errors, mistakes, and perversions which have grown about Will in popular opinion, like those which have accumulated round Christianity, are too often mistaken for the truth. Pure Will is, and must be by its very nature, perfectly *free,* for the more it is hindered, or hampered, or controlled in any way, the less is it independent volition. Therefore, pare Will, free from all restraint can only act in, or as, Moral Law. Acting in accordance with very mean, immoral, obstinate motives is, so to speak, obeying as a slave the devil. The purer the motive the purer the Will, and in very truth the purer the stronger, or firmer. Every man has his own idea of Will according to his morality—even as it is said that every man's conception of God is himself infinitely magnified—or, as SYDNEY SMITH declared, that a certain small clergyman believed that Saint Paul was five feet two inches in height, and wore a shovel-hat. And here we may note that if the fundamental definition of a gentleman be "a man of perfect integrity," or one who always does simply *what is right,* he is also one who possesses Will in its integrity.

Therefore it follows that if the pure will, which is the basis of all firm and determined action, be a matter of moral conviction, it should take the first place as such. Napoleon the First was an exemplar of a selfish corrupted will, CHRIST the perfection of Will in its purity. And if I can make my meaning clear, I would declare that he who would create within himself a strong and vigorous will by hypnotism or any other process, will be most likely to succeed, if, instead of aiming at developing a power by which he may subdue others, and make all things yield to him, or similar selfish aims, he shall, before all, seriously reflect on how he may use it to do good. For I am absolutely persuaded from what I know, that he who makes Altruism and the happiness of others a familiar thought to be coupled with every effort (even as a lamb is always painted with, or appointed unto, St. John), will be the most likely to succeed. There is something in moral conviction or the consciousness of right which gives a sense of security or a faith in success which goes far to secure it. Hence the willing the mind on the following day to be at peace, not to yield to irritability or temptations to quarrel, to be pleasing and cheerful; in short to develop *good* qualities is the most easily effected process, because where there is such self-moral-suasion to a good aim or end, we feel, and very justly, that we *ought* to be aided by the *Deus in nobis,* or an over-ruling Providence, whatever its form or nature may be. And the experimenter may be assured that if we can by any means *will* or exorcise all envy, vanity, folly, irritability, vindictiveness—in short all evil—out of ourselves, and supply their place with Love, we shall take the most effective means to secure our own happiness, as well as that of others.

All of this has been repeated very often of late years by Altruists; but, while the doctrine is accepted both by Agnostics and Christians as perfect, there has been little done to show men how to practically realize it. But I have ever noted that in this Pilgrim's Progress of our life, those are most likely to attain to the Celestial City, and all its golden glories, who, like CHRISTIAN, start from the lowliest beginnings; and as the learning our letters leads to reading the greatest books, so the simplest method of directing the attention and the most mechanical means of developing Will, may promptly lead to the highest mental and moral effect.

Prayer is generally regarded as nothing else but an asking or begging from a superior power. But it is also something which is really very different from this. It is a formula by means of which man realizes his faith and will. Tradition, and habit (of whose power I have spoken) or repetition, have given it the influence or prestige of a charm. In fact it *is* a spell, he who utters it feels assured that if seriously repeated it will be listened to, and that the Power to whom it is addressed will hear it. The Florentines all round me as I write, who repeat daily, *"Pate nostro quis in cell, santi ficeturie nome tumme!"* in words which they do not understand, do not pray for daily bread or anything else in the formula; they only realize that they commune with God, and are being good. An intelligent prayer in this light is the concentration of thought on a subject, or a *definite* realization. Therefore if when *willing* that tomorrow I shall be calm all day or void of irritation, I put the will or wish into a brief and clear form, it will aid me to promptly realize or feel what I want. And it will be a prayer in its reality, addressed to the Unknown Power or to the Will within us—an invocation, or a spell, according to the mind of him who makes it.

Thus a seeker may repeat: "I *will*, earnestly and deeply, that during all tomorrow I may be in a calm and peaceful state of mind. I *will* with all my heart that if irritating or annoying memories or images, or thoughts of any kind are in any way awakened, that they may be promptly forgotten and fade away!"

I would advise that such a formula be got by heart till very familiar, to be repeated, but not mechanically, before falling to sleeps What is of the very utmost importance is that the operator shall feel its meaning and at the same time give it the impulse of Will by the dual process before described. This, if successfully achieved, will not fail (at least with most minds) to induce success.

This formula, or "spell," will be sufficient for some time. When we feel that it is really beginning to have an effect, we may add to it other wishes. That is to say, be it clearly understood, that by repeating the will to be calm and peaceful, day after day, it will assuredly begin to come of itself, even as a pigeon which hath been "tolled" every day at a certain hour to find corn or crumbs in a certain place, will continue to go there even if the food cease. However, you may renew the first formula if you will. Then we may add gradually the wish to be in a bold or courageous frame of mind, so as to face trials, as follows:

"I *will* with all my soul, earnestly and truly, that I may be on the morrow and all the day deeply inspired with courage and energy, with self-confidence and hope! May it lighten my heart and make me heedless of all annoyances and vexations which may arise! Should such come in my way, may I hold them at no more than their real value, or laugh them aside!"

Proceed gradually and firmly through the series, never trying anything new, until the old has fully succeeded. This is essential, for failure leads to discouragement. Then, in time, fully realizing all its deepest meaning, so as to impress the Imagination one may will as follows:

"May my quickness of Perception, or Intuition, aid me in the business which I expect to undertake tomorrow. I *will* that my faculty of grasping at details and understanding their relations shall be active. May it draw from my memory the hidden things which will aid it!"

The artist or literary man, or poet, may in time earnestly will to this effect:

"I desire that my genius, my imagination, the power which enables man to combine and create; the poetic (or artist) spirit, whatever it be, may act in me tomorrow, awakening great thoughts and suggesting for them beautiful forms."

He who expects to appear in public as an orator, as a lawyer pleading a case, or as a witness, will do much to win success, if after careful forethought or reflecting on what it is that he really wants, he will repeat:

"I will that tomorrow I may speak or plead, with perfect self-possession and absence of all timidity or fear!"

Finally, we may after long and earnest reflection on all which I have said, and truly not till then, resolve on the Masterspell to awaken the Will itself in such a form that it will fill our soul, as it were, unto which intent it is necessary to understand what Will really means to us in its purity and integrity. The formula may be:

"I *will* that I may feel inspired with the power, aided by calm determination, to do what I desire, aided by a sense of right and justice to all. May my will be strong and sustain me in all trials. May it inspire that sense of independence of strength which, allied to a pure conscience, is the greatest source of happiness on earth!"

If the reader can master this last, he can by its aid progress infinitely. And with the few spells which I have given he will need no more, since in these lie the knowledge, and key, and suggestion to all which may be required.

Now it will appear clearly to most, that no man can long and steadily occupy himself with such pursuits, without morally benefiting by them in his waking hours, even if auto-hypnotism were all "mere imagination," in the most frivolous sense of the word. For he who will himself not to yield to irritability, can hardly avoid paying attention to the subject, and thinking thereon, check himself when vexed. And as I have said, what we summon by Will ere long remains as Habit, even as the Elves, called by a spell, remain in the Tower.

Therefore it is of *great* importance for all people who take up and pursue to any degree of success this Art or Science, that they shall be actuated by moral and unselfish motives, since achieved with any other intent the end can only be the bringing of evil and suffering into the soul. For as the good by strengthening the Will make themselves promptly better and holier, so he who increases it merely to make others feel his power will become with it wickeder, yea, and thrice accursed, for what is the greatest remedy is often the strongest poison.

Step by step Science has advanced of late to the declaration that man *thinks all over* his body, or at least experiences those reflected sensations or emotions which are so strangely balanced between intellectual sense and sensation that we hardly know where or how to class them. "The sensitive *plexi* of our whole organism are all either isolated or thrown into simultaneous vibration when acted on by Thought." So the Will may be found acting unconsciously as an emotion or instinct, or developed with the highest forms of conscious reflection. Last of all we find it, probably as the result of all associated functions or powers, at the head of all, their Executive president. But *is* it "the exponent of correlated forces?" There indeed doctors differ.

There is a very curious Italian verb, *Invogliare,* which is thus described in a Dictionary of Idioms: *"Invogliare* is to inspire a will or desire, *cupiditatem injicere a movere.* To *invogliare* anyone is to awake in him the will or the ability or capacity, an earnest longing or appetite, an ardent wish—*alicujus rei cupiditatem a desiderium alicni movere*—to bring into action a man's hankering, solicitude, anxiety, yearning, ardor, predilection, love, fondness and relish, or aught which savors of Willing." Our English word, *Inveigle,* is derived from it, but we have none precisely corresponding to it which so generally sets forth the idea of inspiring a will in another person. "Suggestion" is far more general and vague. Now if a man could thus *in-will* himself to good or moral purpose, he would assume a new position in life. We all admit that most human beings have defects or faults of which they would gladly be freed (however incorrigible they *appear to* be), but they have not the patience to effect a cure, to keep to the resolve, or prevent it from fading out of sight. For a *vast* proportion of all minor sins, or those within the law, there is no cure sought. The offender says and believes, "It is too strong for me"—and yet these small unpunished offenses cause a thousand times more suffering than all the great crimes.

Within a generation, owing to the great increase of population, prosperity and personal comfort, nervous susceptibility has also gained in extent, but there has been no check to petty abuse of power, selfishness, which always comes out in some form of injustice or wrong, or similar vexations. Nay, what with the disproportionate growth of vulgar wealth, this element has rapidly increased, and it would really seem as if the plague must spread *ad infinitum*, unless some means can be found to *invogliare* and inspire the offenders with a sense of their sins, and move them to reform. And it is more than probable that if all who are at heart sincerely willing to reform their morals and manners could be brought to keep their delinquencies before their consciousness in the very simple manner which I have indicated, the fashion or *mode* might at least be inaugurated. For it is *not* so much a moral conviction, or an appeal to common sense, which is needed (as writers on ethics all seem to think), but some practical art of keeping men up to the mark in endeavoring to reform, or to make them remember it all day long, since "out of sight out of mind" is the devil's greatest help with weak minds.

CHAPTER VI.

SUGGESTION AND INSTINCT.

"Anima non nascitur sed fit," ut ait.—TERTULLIANUS.

"Post quam loquuti sumus de anima rationali, intellectuali
(immortali) et quia ad inferiores descendimus jam gradus
animæ, scilicet animæ mortalis quæ animalium est."
—PETRUS GREGORIUS THOLOSANUS.

It must have struck many readers that the action of a mind under hypnotic influence, be it of another or of self, involves strange questions as regards Consciousness. For it is very evident from recorded facts, that people can actually reason and act without waking consciousness, in a state of mind which resembles instinct, which is a kind of cerebration, or acting under habits and impressions supplied by memory and formed by practice, but not according to what we understand by Reason or Judgment.

All things in nature have their sleep or rest, night is the sleep of the world, death the repose of Nature or Life—the solid temples, the great globe itself, dissolve to awaken again; so man hath in him, as it were, a company of workmen, some of whom labor by day, while others watch by night, during which time they, unseen, have their fantastic frolics known as dreams. The Guardian or Master of the daily hours, appears in a great measure to conform his action closely to average duties of life, in accordance with those of all other men. He picks out from the millions of images or ideas in the memory, uses and becomes familiar with a certain number, and lets the rest sleep. This master or active agent is probably himself a Master-Idea—the result of the correlative action of all the others, a kind of consensus made personal, an elected Queen Bee, as I have otherwise described him or her.

But he is not the only thinker—there are all over the body ganglions which act by a kind of fluid instinct, born of repetition, and when the tired master even drowses or nods, or falls into a brown study, then a marvelously curious mental action begins to show itself, for dreams at once flicker and peer and steal dimly about him. This is because the waking consciousness is beginning to shut out the world—and its set of ideas.

So consistent is the system that even if Waking Reason abstract itself, not to sleep, but to think on one subject such as writing a poem or inventing a machine, certain affinities will sleep or dreams begin to show themselves. When Genius is really at work, it sweeps along, as it were, in a current, albeit it has enough reason left to also use the rudder and oars, or spread and manage a sail. The reason for the greater fullness of unusual images and associations (*i. e.*, the action of genius) during the time when one is bent on intellectual invention is that the more the waking conscious Reason drowses or approaches to sleep, the more do many images in Memory awaken and begin to shyly open the doors of their cells and peep out.

In the dream we also proceed, or rather drift, loosely on a current, but are without oars, rudder or sail. We are hurtled against, or hurried away from the islands of Images or Ideas, that is to say, all kinds of memories, and our course is managed or impelled, or guided by tricky water-sprites, whose minds are all on mischief bent or only idle merriment. In any case they conduct us blindly and wildly from isle to isle, sometimes obeying a far cry which comes to them through the mist—some echoing signal of our waking hours. So in a vision ever on we go!

That is to say that even while we dream there is an unconscious cerebration or voluntarily exerted power loosely and irregularly imitating by habit, something like the action of our waking hours, especially its brown studies and fancies in drowsy reveries or play.

It seems to me as if this sleep-master or mistress—I prefer the latter—who attends to our dreams may be regarded as Instinct on the loose, for like instinct she acts without conscious reasoning. She carries out, or realizes, trains of thought, or sequences with little comparison or deduction. Yet within her limits she can do great work, and when we consider, we shall find that by following mere Law she has effected a great, nay, an immense, deal, which we attribute entirely to forethought or Reason. As all this is closely allied to the action of the mind when hypnotized, it deserves further study.

Now it is a wonderful reflection that as we go back in animated nature from man to insects, we find self-conscious Intellect or Reason based on Reflection disappear, and Instinct taking its place. Yet Instinct in its marvelous results, such as ingenuity of adaptation, often far surpasses what semi-civilized man could do. Or it does the same things as man, only in an entirely different way which is not as yet understood. Only from time to time some one tells a wonderful story of a bird, a dog or a cat, and then asks, "Was not this reason?"

What it was, in a great measure, was an unconscious application of memory or experience. Bees and ants and birds often far outdo savage men in ingenuity of construction. The red Indians in their persistent use of flimsy, cheerless bark wigwams, were far behind the beaver or oriole as regards dwellings; in this respect the Indian indicated mere instinct of a low order, as all do who live in circles of mere tradition.

Now to advance what seems a paradox, it is evident that even what we regard as inspired genius comes to man in a great measure from Instinct, though as I noted before it is aided by reflection. As the young bird listens to its mother and then sings till as a grown nightingale it pours forth a rich flood of varying melody; so the poet or musician follows masters and models, and then, like them, *creates*, often progressing, but is never *entirely* spontaneous or original. When the artist thinks too little he lacks sense, when he thinks too much he loses fire. In the very highest and most strangely mysterious poetical flights of SHELLEY and KEATS, or WORDSWORTH, I find the very same Instinct which inspires the skylark and nightingale, but more or less allied to and strengthened by Thought or Consciousness. If human Will or Wisdom alone directed *all* our work, then every man who had mere patience might be a great original genius, and it is indeed true that Man can do inconceivably more in following and imitating genius than has ever been imagined. However, thus far the talent which enables a man to write such a passage as that of TENNYSON,

> "The tides of Music's golden sea
> Setting towards Eternity,"

results from a development of Instinct, or an intuitive perception of the Beautiful, such as Wordsworth believed existed in all things which enjoy sunshine, *life*, and air. The poet himself cannot *explain* the processes, though he may be able to analyze in detail how or why he made or found a thousand other things.

It is not only true that Genius originates in something antecedent to conscious reflection or intellect, but also that men have produced marvelous works of art almost without knowing it, while others have shown the greatest incapacity to do so after they had developed an incredible amount of knowledge. Thus Mr. WHISTLER reminded RUSKIN that when the world had its greatest artists, there were no critics.

And it is well to remember that while the Greeks in all their glory of Art and Poetry were unquestionably rational or consciously intelligent, there was not among them the thousandth part of the anxious worrying, the sentimental self-seeking and examination, or the Introversion which worms itself in and out of, and through and through, all modern work, action and thought, even as mercury in an air-pump will permeate the hardest wood. For the Greeks worked more in the spirit of Instinct; that is, more according to certain transmitted laws and ideas than we realize—albeit this tradition was of a very high order. We have lost Art because we have not developed tradition, but have immensely increased consciousness, or reflection, out of proportion to art It was from India and Egypt in a *positive* form that Man drew the poison of sentimental Egoism which became comparative in the Middle Ages and superlative in this our time.

It is very evident that as soon as men become self-conscious of great work, or cease to work for the sake of enjoying Art, or its results, and turn all their attention to the genius or cleverness, or character or style, self, *et cetera*, of the *artist*, or of themselves, a decadence sets in, as there did after the Renaissance, when knowledge or enjoyment of Art was limited, and guided by familiarity with names and schools and "manners," or the like, far more than by real beauty in itself.

Now, out of all this which I have said on Art, strange conclusions may be drawn, the first being that even without self-conscious Thought or excess of Intellect, there can be a Sense of Enjoyment in any or every organism, also a further development of memory of that enjoyment, and finally a creation of buildings, music and song, with no reflection, in animals, and very little in Man. And when Man gets beyond working with simple Nature and begins to think chiefly about himself, his Art, as regards harmony with Nature, deteriorates.

We do not sufficiently reflect on the fact that *Natura naturans*, or the action of Nature (or simply following Tradition), may, as is the case of Transition Architecture, involve the creation of marvelously ingenious and beautiful works, and the great enjoyment of them by Instinct alone. It is not possible for ordinary man to even understand this now in all its fullness. He is indeed trying to do so—but it is too new for his comprehension. But a time will come when he will perceive that his best work has been done unconsciously, or under influences of which he was ignorant.

Hypnotism acts entirely by suggestion, and he who paints or does other work entirely according to Tradition, also carries out what is or has been suggested to him. Men of earlier times who thus worked for thousands of years like the Egyptians in one style, were guided by the faith that it had been begun by the Creator or God.

For men cannot conceive of creation as separate from pre-determined plan or end, and all because they cannot understand that Creative innate force, *potentia*, must have some result, or that the simplest Law once set agoing awakens, acquires strength in going and develops great Laws, which, with an all-susceptible or *capable* material to work on, may, or *must*, create infinite ingenuities, so that in time there may be an organic principle with sentiency, and yet no Will, save in its exponents, or working to end or aim, but ever tending to further unfolding "a seizing and giving the fire of the living" ever onwards into Eternity, in which there may be a million times more perfect "mind" than we can now grasp.

Now, having for many years attempted at least to familiarize myself with the aspect or sound, of this problem, though I could not solve it, it seems at last to be natural enough that even matter (which so many persist in regarding as a kind of dust or something resistant to the touch, but which I regard as infinite millions of degrees more subtle), may *think* just as well as it may act in Instinct. It is, indeed, absurd to admit souls to idiots or savages, who have not the sense to live as comfortably as many animals, and yet deny it to the latter. When we really become familiar with the idea, it appears sensible enough. But its opponents do *not* become familiar with it, it irritates them, they call it Atheistic, although it is nothing of the kind, just as if we were to say that a man who bravely and nobly pursued his way in life, doing his duty because it was his duty, and giving no thought as to future reward or punishment, must needs want *soul* or be an Atheist.

If all men were perfectly good, they would act morally and instinctively, without consciousness of behaving well, and if we felt a high ideal of Art it would be just the same. When Art was natural men never signed their names to their work, but now the Name takes precedence of the picture.

Therefore, as we go backward into the night of things, we find, though we forget it all the time, that Instinct or the living in the Spirit of Law, had its stars or planets which shone more brilliantly than now, at least in Faith. Thus, there are two sources of Creation or Action, both based on Evolution, one being unconscious and guided by Natural Law, and the other which is conscious and grows out of the first. Hence *cognito ergo sum,* which well-nigh all men really understand as *cogito, ergo sum Deus.* Or we may say that they assume

"Because *I* think, then God must *think* like me!"

Now to come to Hypnotic thought, or suggested mental action. I would infer that, according to what I have said, there may be two kinds of mentality, or working of the mind—the one under certain conditions as effective or resultant as the other; the first being—as it was in the order of time—Unconscious or Instinctive; the other, conscious and self-observant.

For the man who built a Romanesque Cathedral worked by the suggestiveness of minds which went before him, or Tradition. He was truly, as it were, in a kind of slumber; indeed, all life was more or less of a waking dream in those dim, strange days. "Millions marched forth to death scarce knowing why," all because they were *told* to do so—they felt that they must do it, and they did it. "Like turkeys led by a red rag," says CARLYLE. And the red rag and the turkey is an illustration of Hypnotism in one of the books thereon. Instinct *is* Hypnotism.

Now I have found that by suggesting to oneself before sleep, or inducing self by Will or Forethought to work gladly and unweariedly the next day, we do not *think* about self or the quality of what we do to any degree like what we would in working under ordinary conditions. Truly it is not thoroughgoing or infallible in all cases, but *then* it must be helped by a little wide-awake self-conscious will. But this is certainly true, that we can turn out *better* work when we urge our creative power to awake in the morn and act or aid, than if we do not.

"For there are many angels at our call,
And many blessed spirits who are bound
To lend their aid in every strait and turn;
And elves to fly the errands of the soul,
And fairies all too glad to give us help,
If we but know how to pronounce the spell
Which calls them unto us in every need."

That spell I have shown or explained clearly enough.

And, finally, to recapitulate, Instinct in its earlier or simpler form is the following laws of Nature which are themselves formed by motive laws. In Man the living according to Tradition is instinct of a higher order, and the one or the other is merely being ruled by Suggestion. The more free Will is developed and guided by reflection, or varied tradition and experience, the less instinct and the more intellect will there be.

CHAPTER VII.

MEMORY CULTURE.

> 'Twas wisely said by Plato, when he called
> Memory "the mother of the Intellect,"
> For knowledge is to wisdom what his realm
> Is to a monarch—that o'er which he rules;
> And he who hath the Will can ever win
> Such empire to himself—Will can do all.

There is nothing in which the might of the Will can be so clearly set forth as in the *making* of memory. By means of it, as is fully proved by millions of examples, man can render his power of recollection almost infinite. And lest the reader may think that I here exaggerate, I distinctly assert that I never knew a man of science, familiar with certain facts which I shall repeat, who ever denied its literal truth.

As I have already stated, there are two methods, and only two, by means of which we can retain images, facts or ideas. One of these is that which in many varied forms, which are all the same in fact, is described in the old *Artes Memorandi,* or Arts of Memory. There are several hundreds of these, and to the present day there are professors who give instructions according to systems of the same kind. These are all extremely plausible, being based on Association of ideas, and in most cases the pupil makes great progress for a short time. Thus, we can remember the French for bread, *pain,* Italian *Pane,* by thinking of the *pan* in which bread is baked, or the difficult name of the inventor, SSCZEPANIK (pronounced nearly *she-panic*) by thinking of a crowd of frightened women, and which I remembered by the fact that *pane* is the Slavonian for Mr. or Sir. For there is such a tendency of ideas to agglutinate, and so become more prominent, as we can see two bubbles together in a pool more readily than one that we can very soon learn to recall many images in this way.

But after a time a certain limit is reached which most minds cannot transgress. VOLAPUK was easy so long as, like Pidgin-English, it contained only a few hundred words and no grammar. But now that it has a dictionary of 4,000 terms and a complete grammar it is as hard to learn as Spanish. It invariably comes to pass in learning to remember by the Associative method that after a time images are referred to images, and these to others again, so that they form entire categories in which the most vigorous mind gets lost.

The other method is that of *direct* Memory guided by Will, in which no regard is paid to Association, especially in the beginning. Thus to remember anything, or rather to learn *how* to do so, we take something which is very easy to retain—the easier the better—be it a jingling nursery rhyme, a proverb, or a text. Let this be learned to perfection, backwards and forwards, or by permutation of words, and repeated the next day. Note that the repetition or *reviewing* is of more importance than aught else.

On the second day add another proverb or verse to the preceding, and so on, day by day, always reviewing and never learning another syllable until you are sure that you perfectly or most familiarly retain all which you have *memorized*. The result will be, if you persevere, that before long you will begin to find it easier to remember anything. This is markedly the case as regards the practice of reviewing, which is invariably hard at first, but which becomes ere long habitual and then easy.

I cannot impress it too vividly on the mind of the reader, that he cannot make his exercises too easy. If he finds that ten lines a day are too much, let him reduce them to five, or two, or one, or even a single word, but learn that, and persevere. When the memory begins to improve under this process, the tasks may, of course, be gradually increased.

An uncle of the present Khedive of Egypt told me that when he was learning English, he at first committed to memory fifty words a day, but soon felt himself compelled to very much reduce the number in order to permanently remember what he acquired. One should never overdrive a willing horse.

Where there is a teacher with youthful pupils, he can greatly aid the process of mere memorizing, by explaining the text, putting questions as to its meaning, or otherwise awaking an interest in it. After a time the pupils may proceed to *verbal memorizing,* which consists of having the text simply read or repeated to them. In this way, after a year or eighteen months of practice, most people can actually remember a sermon or lecture, word for word.

This was the process which was discovered, I may say simultaneously, by DAVID KAY and myself, as our books upon it appeared at almost the same time. But since then I have modified my plan, and made it infinitely easier, and far more valuable, as will be apparent to all, by the application of the principles laid down in this book. For while, according to the original views, Memory depended on Will and Perseverance, there was no method indicated by any writer how these were to be created, nor was energetic Forethought considered as amounting to more than mere Intention.

Now I would say that having the task selected, first give energetic forethought, or a considerate determination to master this should precede all attempts to learn, by everybody, young or old. And when the lesson is mastered, let it be repeated with earnestness and serious attention before going to sleep, with the *Will* that it shall be remembered on the morrow. And it will be found that this process not only secures the memory desired, but also greatly facilitates the whole course and process.

It is to be noted that by this, or any process, we do not remember everything, but only what is first considered and measured by Forethought. Also that by it the Memory is never overcharged at the expense of Intellect, for the exertion of will in any way strengthens the mind. To explain the immense power which this all implies, I observe:

That previous to the invention of printing, it was usual for students to get their text-books by heart. Thus in India, according to MAX MULLER, the entire text and glosses of PANINI'S Sanskrit grammar were handed down orally for 350 years before being committed to writing. This work is about equal in size to the Bible.

There are Indian priests now living who can repeat accurately the whole poems of the *Mahabarata* of 300,000 *slokas* or lines.

That these incredible feats were the result of a system of memorizing similar to what I have explained.

That the *Guzlas* or Slavonian minstrels of the present day have by heart with remarkable accuracy immensely long epic poems. I have found the same among Algonkin Indians, whose sagas or mythic legends are interminable, and yet are committed word by word accurately.

I have heard in England of a lady ninety years of age whose memory was miraculous, and of which extraordinary instances are narrated by her friends. She attributed it to the fact that when young she had been made to learn a verse from the Bible every day, and then constantly review it. As her memory improved, she learned more, the result being that in the end she could repeat from memory any verse or chapter called for in the whole Scripture. The habit had marvelously developed her intelligence as well as memory.

Now I confidently declare that if this lady had submitted what she learned to the suggestive-will process she could have spared herself half the labor. And it is to be observed that as in time the labor of reviewing and the faculty of promptly recalling becomes easier and easier till it is simply mechanical, so the memorizing by suggestion becomes more *facile* until it is, so to speak, only a form. And as it becomes easier the foresight strengthens till it wields an *absolute* power.

If the reader is interested in this subject of developing the memory, I would refer him to my work on Practical Education in which it is discussed with reference to recalling objects through all the Senses.

No one who has made even a very slight trial of the process of impressing on the mind before sleep something which must be remembered, can fail to be convinced ere long of the truth that there is in it a marvelous power which will with easy and continued practice enable him to recall whatever he pleases. It follows as a matter of course, that this would be of incredible value in education, but notwithstanding the vast discussion of this subject which is ever going on, it does not seem to occur to a living man that we should develop and train the mental faculties, such as memory and quickness of perception, as well as set them to hard work.

It is also safe to say that there is not a man living who was educated from boyhood upon this principle, and yet I am confident that no scientist in existence, knowing the facts on which my statement is based, will deny that it is as easy to develop the mental factors alluded to, as to learn a language or play on the piano. It is not a matter of theory but of facts. Millions of men have in the past acquired the faculty of being able to repeat and remember whatever they heard, if they earnestly attended to it. Earnest attention in this case means a strong exercise of forethought, or determination to an end or given purpose. In Iceland, that which has since become the English common law, was at an early date very fully developed, without any books or writing. And there were lawyers who had by heart all the laws, and incredible numbers of precedents, as appears from several sagas, among others, that of The Burnt Njall.

Our present system of Education is that of building houses without foundations. No one suspects or dreams what mighty powers there are latent in us all, or how easily they may be developed. It would not be so reprehensible if men entirely neglected the subject, but they are always working hard and spending millions on the old system, and will not even make the least experiment to test a new theory. One reason for this is the old belief that we are all born with a certain quantum of "gifts," as for example memory, capacity, patience, *et cetera,* all more or less limited, and in reality not to be enlarged or improved. The idea is *natural*, because we see that there are very great differences, hereditary or otherwise, in children. But it is false. So we go to work to fill up the quantum of memory as soon as possible by violent cramming, and in like manner tax to the utmost all the mental faculties without making the least effort to prepare, enlarge or strengthen them.

I shall not live to see it, but a time will come when this preparation of the mental faculties will be regarded as the basis of all education.

To recapitulate in a few words. When we desire to fix anything in the memory we can do so by repeating it to ourselves before we go to sleep, accompanying it with the resolution to remember it in future. We must not in the beginning set ourselves any but very easy tasks, and the practice must be steadily continued.

It has been often said that a perfect memory is less of a blessing than the power of oblivion. Thus THEMISTOCLES (who, according to CATO, as cited by CICERO, knew the names and faces of every man in Athens) having offered to teach some one the art of memory, received for reply, "Rather teach me how to forget"—*esse facturum si se oblivisci quæ vellet, quam si meminisse docuisset.* And CLAUDIUS had such an enviable power in the latter respect that immediately after he had put to death his wife MESSALINA, he forgot all about it, asking, *"Cur domina non veniret?"*—"Why the Missus didn't come?"—while on the following day, after condemning several friends to death, he sent invitations to them to come and dine with him. And again, there are people who have, as it were, two memories, one good, the other bad, as was the case with CALVISIUS SABRINUS, who could recall anything in literature, but never remembered the names of his own servants, or even his friends. But he got over the difficulty by naming his nine attendants after the nine Muses, while he called his intimates Homer, Hesiod, and so on. This scholar would truly seem to have drunk of the two fountains sacred to Trophonius, by the river Orchomenus in Bœotia, one of which bestowed memory and the other oblivion. And like unto them is the power of the Will, aided by Forethought and Suggestion, for while it properly directs and aids us to remember what we will, it *per contra* also helps us to forget.

CHAPTER VIII.

THE CONSTRUCTIVE FACULTIES.

> "He who hath learned a single art,
> Can thrive, I ween, in any part."
>   —*German Proverb.*

> "He would have taught you how you might employ
> Yourself; and many did to him repair,
> And, certes, not in vain; he had inventions rare."
>   —WORDSWORTH.

When I had, after many years of study and research in England and on the Continent, developed the theory that all practical, technical education of youth should be preceded by a light or easy training on an æsthetic basis, or the minor arts, I for four years, to test the scheme, was engaged in teaching in the city of Philadelphia, every week in separate classes, two hundred children, besides a number of ladies. These were from the public schools of the city. The total number of these public pupils was then 110,000.

My pupils were taught, firstly, simple outline decorative design with drawing at the same time; after this, according to sex, easy embroidery, wood carving, modeling in clay, leather-work, carpentering, inlaying, repoussé modeling in clay, porcelain painting, and other small arts. Nearly all of the pupils, who were from ten to sixteen years of age, acquired two or three, if not all, of these arts, and then very easily found employment in factories or fabrics, etc.

Many people believed that this was all waste of money and time, and, quite unknown to me, at their instigation an inquiry was made of all the teachers in the public schools as to the standing of my art pupils in their other classes, it being confidently anticipated that they would be found to have fallen behind. And the result of the investigation was that the two hundred were in advance of the one hundred and ten thousand in every branch—geography, arithmetic, history, and so on.

It was not remarkable, because boys and girls who had, at an average age of twelve or thirteen, learned the principles of design and its practical application to several kinds of handiwork, and knew the differences and characteristics of Gothic, Arabesque, or Greek patterns, all developed a far greater intelligence in general thought and conversation than others. They had at least one topic on which they could converse intelligently with any grown-up person, and in which they were really superior to most. They soon found this out. I have often been astonished in listening to their conversation among themselves to hear how well they discussed art. They all well knew at least one thing, which is far from being known among æsthetes in London, which is that in Decorative Art, however you may end in all kinds of mixtures of styles, you must at least begin with organic development, and not put roots or flowers at *both* ends of a branch or vine.

The secret of it all is that those who from an early age develop the constructive faculty (especially if this be done in a pleasing, easy manner, with agreeable work) also develop with it the Intellect, and that very rapidly to a very remarkable degree. There are reasons for this. Drawing when properly taught stimulates visual perception or eye memory; this is strikingly the case when the pupil has a model placed in one room, and, after studying it, goes into another room to reproduce it from memory. Original design, which when properly taught is learned with incredible ease by all children, stimulates observation to a remarkable degree. The result of such education is to develop a great general quickness of perception and thought.

Now, be it observed, that if anyone desires to learn design or any art, it may be greatly facilitated by the application to it of Will and Foresight, and in the beginning, Self-Suggestion. He who understands the three as one, sees in it a higher or more energetic kind of self-discipline than most people practise. In the end they come to the same as a vigorous effort of the Will.

Thus, having mastered the very easy principles of design which govern all organic development or vegetable growth (as set forth in a plant with roots, offshoots, or crochets, and end ornaments, flowers, or finials, with the circle, spiral, and offshooting ornaments; rings made into vines and wave patterns; all of which can be understood in an hour with diagrams), let the beginner attempt a design, the simpler the better, and reproduce it from memory. If on going to bed he will impress it on his mind that on the morrow he would like to make more designs, or that it *must* be done, he will probably feel the impulse and succeed. This is the more likely because patterns impress themselves very vividly on the memory or imagination, and when studied are easily recalled after a little practice.

The manner in which most artists form an idea, or project their minds to a plan or invention, be it a statue or picture; and the way they think it over and anticipate it—very often actually seeing the picture in a finished state in imagination—all amounts to foresight and hypnotic preparation in a crude, imperfect form. If any artist who is gifted with resolution and perseverance will simply make trial of the method here recommended, he will assuredly find that it is a great aid to Invention.

It is probable that half the general average cleverness of men is due to their having learned, as boys, games, or the art of making something, or mending and repairing. In any case, if they had learned to use their hands and their inventiveness or adaptability, they would have been the better for it. That the innumerable multitude of people who can do nothing of the kind, and who take no real interest in anything except spending money and gossiping, are to be really pitied, is true. Some of them once had minds—and these are the most pitiful or pitiable of all. It is to be regretted that novels are, with rare exceptions, written to amuse this class, and limit themselves strictly to "life," never describing with real skill, so as to interest anything which would make life worth living for—except love—which is good to a certain extent, but not absolutely all in all, save to the eroto-maniac. And as most novelists now pretend to instruct and convey ideas, beyond mere story-telling, or even being "interesting," which means the love or detective business, I would suggest to some of these writers that the marvelous latent powers of the human mind, and also some art which does not consist of the names and guide-book praises of a few great painters and the Renaissance *rechauffée* would be a refreshing novelty.

The ancient Romans were thoroughly persuaded that *Exercitatione et usu* (by exercising the physical faculties in every way; by which they meant arts as well as gymnastics; and by making such practice habitual) they could develop intellect, in illustration of which Lycurgus once took two puppies of the same litter, and had the one brought up to hunt, while the other was nursed at home in all luxury; and when grown, and let loose, the one caught a hare, while the other yelped and ran away. So the word *handy,* in old English *hend,* meaning quick, alert, or gifted with prompt perception, is derived from knowing how to use the hands. BRUSONIUS ("Facetiæ," Lyons, 1562) has collected a great number of classic anecdotes to illustrate this saying.

Recapitulation. Those who desire to become artists, can greatly facilitate their work, if beginning for example with very simple outline decorative designs, and having learned the principles on which they are constructed, they would repeat or revise them to themselves before sleep, resolving to remember them. The same principle is applicable to all kinds of designs, with the proviso that they be at first very easy. This is generally a very successful process.

Fore thought, or the projection of conception or attention with will, is a marvelous preparation for all kinds of art work. He who can form the habit of seeing a picture mentally before he paints it, has an incredible advantage, and will spare himself much labor and painting out.

CHAPTER IX.

FASCINATION.

> "Quærit *Franciscus Valesius, Delrio, Gutierrus,* et alii,
> unde vulgaris ilia fascini nata sit opinio de oculo fascinante
> visione et ore fascinando laudando."—De Faseinatione
> Fatatus. A. D. 1677.

I have in Chapter Fifth mentioned several of the subjects to attain which the Will may be directed by the aid of self-hypnotism, preceded by Forethought. If the reader has carefully studied what I have said and not merely skimmed it, he must have perceived that if the power be fully acquired, it makes, as it were, new existence for its possessor, opening to him boundless fields of action by giving him the enviable power to acquire interest—that is to say agreeable or profitable occupation—in whatever he pleases. In further illustration of which I add the following:

To recall bygone memories or imperfectly remembered sensations, scenes and experiences or images.

This is a difficult thing to describe, and no wonder, since it forms the greatest and most trying task of all poets to depict that which really depends for its charm on association, emotion and a chiaroscuro of the feelings. We have all delightful reminiscences which make ridiculous Dante's assertion that

"There is no greater grief than to recall in pain
The happy days gone by;"

which, if true, would make it a matter of regret that we ever had a happy hour. However, I assume that it is a great pleasure to recall, even in grief, beautiful bygone scenes and joys, and trust that the reader has a mind healthy and cheerful enough to do the same.

What constitutes a charm in many memories is often extremely varied. Darkly shaded rooms with shutters closed in on an intensely hot American summer day. Chinese matting on the floors—the mirrors and picture frames covered with *tulle*—silence—the scent of magnolias all over the house—the presence of loved ones now long dead and gone—all of these combined form to me memory-pictures in which nothing can be spared. The very scent of the flowers is like musk in a perfume or "bouquet" of odors—it *fixes* them well, or renders them permanent. And it is all like a beautiful vivid dream. If I had my life to live over again I would do frequently and with great care, what I thought of too late, and now practice feebly—I would strongly impress on my mind and very often recall, many such scenes, pictures, times or memories. Very few people do this. Hence in all novels and poems, especially the French, description generally smacks of imitation and mere manufacture. It passes for "beautiful writing," but there is always something in really unaffected truth from nature which is caught by the true critic. I read lately a French romance which is much admired, of this manufactured or second-hand kind. Every third page was filled with the usual botany, rocks, skies, colors, fore and backgrounds—"all very fine"—but in the whole of it not one of those little touches of truth which stir us so in SHAKESPEARE, make us smile in HERRICK or naïve PEPYS, or raise our hearts in WORDSWORTH. These were true men.

To be true we must be far more familiar with Nature than with scene painting or photographs, and to do this we must, so to speak, fascinate ourselves with pictures in life, glad memories of golden hours, rock and river and greenwood tree. We must also banish resolutely from our past all recollections of enemies and wrongs, troubles and trials, and throw all our heart into doing so. Forgive and forget all enmities—those of Misfortune and Fate being included. Depend upon it that the brighter you can make your Past the pleasanter will be your Future.

This is just the opposite to what most people do, hence the frequent and fond quotation of pessimistic poetry. It is all folly, and worse. One result is that in modern books of travel the only truthful or vivid descriptions are of sufferings of all kinds, even down to inferior luncheons and lost hair brushes. Their joys they sketch with an indifferent skill, like HEINE'S monk, who made rather a poor description of Heaven, but was "gifted in Hell," which he depicted with dreadful vigor.

I find it a great aid to recall what I can of bygone beautiful associations, and then sleep on them with a resolve that they shall recur in complete condition. He who will thus resolutely clean up his past life and clear away from it all sorrow *as well as he can,* and refurnish it with beautiful memories, or make it better, *coûte que coûte,* will do himself more good than many a doleful moral adviser ever dreamed of. This is what I mean by *self-fascination*—the making, as it were, by magic art, one's own past and self more charming than we ever deemed it possible to be. We thus fascinate ourselves. Those who believe that everything which is bygone has gone to the devil are in a wretched error. The future is based on the past—yes, made from it, and that which *was* never dies, but returns to bless or grieve. We mostly wrong our past bitterly, and bitterly does it revenge itself. But it is like the lion of ANDROCLES, it remembers those who treat it kindly. "And lo! when ANDROCLES was thrown to the lion to be devoured, the beast lay down at his feet, and licked his hands." Yes, we have all our lions!

To master difficult meanings. It has often befallen me, when I was at the University, or later when studying law, to exert my mind to grasp, and all in vain, some problem in mathematics or a puzzling legal question, or even to remember some refractory word in a foreign language which would *not* remain in the memory. After a certain amount of effort in many of these cases, further exertion is injurious, the mind or receptive power seems to be seized—as if nauseated—with spasmodic rejections. In such a case pass the question by, but on going to bed, think it over and *will* to understand it on the morrow. It will often suffice to merely desire that it shall recur in more intelligible form—in which case, *nota bene*—if let alone it will obey. This is as if we had a call to make tomorrow, when, as we know, the memory will come at its right time of itself, especially if we employ Forethought or special pressure.

When I reflect on what I once endured from this cause, and how greatly it could have been relieved or alleviated, I feel as if I could beg, with all my heart, every student or teacher of youth to seriously experiment on what I set forth in this book. It is also to be observed, especially by metaphysicians and mental philosophers, that a youth who has shown great indifference to, let us say mathematics, if he has manifested an aptitude for philosophy or languages, will be in all cases certain to excel in the former, if he can be brought to make a good beginning in it. A great many cases of bad, *i. e.,* indifferent scholarship, are due to bad teaching of the rudiments by adults who took no *interest* in their pupils, and therefore inspired none.

To determine what course to follow in any Emergency. Many a man often wishes with all his heart that he had some wise friend to consult in his perplexities. What to do in a business trouble when we are certain that there is an exit if we could only find it—a sure way to tame an unruly horse if we had the secret—to do or not to do whate'er the question—truly all this causes great trouble in life. But, it is within the power of man to be his own friend, yes, and companion, to a degree of which none have ever dreamed, and which borders on the *weird*, or that which forebodes or suggests mysteries to come. For it may come to pass that he who has trained himself to it, may commune with his spirit as with a companion.

This is, of course, done by just setting the problem, or question, or dilemma, before ourselves as clearly as we can, so as to know our own minds as well as possible. This done, sleep on it, with the resolute will to have it recur on the morrow in a clear and solved form. And should this occur, do not proceed to pull it to pieces again, by way of improvement, but rather submit it to another night's rest. I would here say that many lawyers and judges are perfectly familiar with this process, and use it habitually, without being aware of its connection with hypnotism or will. But they could aid it, if they would add this peculiar *impulse* to the action.

What I will now discuss approaches the miraculous, or seems to do so because it has been attempted or treated in manifold ways by sorcerers and witches. The Voodoos, or black wizards in America, profess to be able to awaken love in one person for another by means of incantations, but admit that it is the most difficult of their feats. Nor do I think that there is any infallible recipe for it, but that there are means of *honestly* aiding such affection can hardly be denied. In the first place, he who would be loved must love—for that is no honest love which is not sincere. And having thus inspired himself, and made himself as familiar as possible, by quietly observing as dispassionately as may be all the mental characteristics of the one loved, let him with an earnest desire to know how to secure a return, go to sleep, and see whether the next day will bring a suggestion. And as the old proverb declares that luck comes to many when least hoped for, so will it often happen that forethought is thus fore-bought or secured.

It is known that gifts pass between friends or lovers, to cause the receiver to think of the giver, thus they are in a sense amulets. If we believe, as HEINE prettily suggests, that something of the life or the being of the owner or wearer has passed into the talisman, we are not far off from the suggestion that our feelings are allied. All over Italy, or over the world, pebbles of precious stone, flint or amber, rough topaz or agate, are esteemed as lucky; all things of the kind lead to suggestiveness, and may be employed in suggestion.

What was originally known as Fascination, of which the German, FROMANN, wrote a very large volume which I possess, is simply Hypnotism without the putting to sleep. It is direct Suggestion. Where there is a natural sympathy of like to like, soul answering soul, such suggestion is easily established. Among people of a common, average, worldly type who are habitually sarcastic, jeering, chaffing, and trifling, or those whose idea of genial or agreeable companionship is to "get a rise" out of all who will give and take irritations equally, there can be no sympathy of gentle or refined emotions. Experiments, whose whole nature presupposes earnest thought, cannot be tried with any success by those who live habitually in an atmosphere of small talk and "rubbishy" associations. Fascination should be mutual; to attempt to exert it on anyone who is not naturally in sympathy is a crime, and I believe that all such cases lead to suffering and remorse.

But where we perceive that there is an undoubted mutual liking and good reason for it, fascination, when perfectly understood and sympathetically used, facilitates and increases love and friendship, and may be most worthily and advantageously employed. Unto anyone who could, for example, merely skim over all that I have written, catching an idea here and there, and then expect to master all, I can clearly say that I can give him or her no definite idea of fascination. For Fascination really is effectively what the old philosophers, who had given immense study and research to the subject in ages when susceptibility to suggestiveness went far beyond anything now known, all knew and declared; that is to say, it existed, but that it required a peculiar mind, and very certainly one which is not frivolous, to understand its nature, and much more to master it.

He who has by foresight, or previous consideration of a subject or desire, allied to a vigorous resolution (which is a kind of projection of the mind by will—and then submitting it to sleep), learned how to bring about a wished-for state of mind, has, in a curious manner, made as it were of his hidden self a conquest yet a friend. He has brought to life within himself a Spirit, gifted with greater powers than those possessed by Conscious Intellect. By his astonishing and unsuspected latent power, Man can *imagine* and then create, even a spirit within the soul. We make at first the sketch, then model it in clay, then cast it in gypsum, and finally sculpture it in marble.

I read lately, in a French novel, a description of a young lady, by herself, in which she assumed to have within her two souls, one good, of which she evidently thought very little, and another brilliantly diabolical, capricious, vividly dramatic and interesting *esprit*—to which she gave a great deal of attention. He who will begin by merely *imagining* that he has within him a spirit of beauty and light, which is to subdue and extinguish the other or all that is in him of what is low, commonplace, and mean, may bring this idea to exert a marvelous influence. He can increase the conception, and give it reality, by treating it with forethought and will, by suggestion, until it gives marvellous result. This better self may be regarded as a guardian angel, in any case it is a power by means of which we can learn mysteries. It is also our Conscience, born of the perception of Ideals.

The Ideal or Spirit thus evolved should be morally pure, else the experimenter will find, as did the magicians of old, that all who dealt with any but good spirits, fell into the hands of devils, just as ALLAN KARDEC says is the case with Spiritualists. But to speak as clearly as I can, he who succeeds in winning or creating a higher Self within himself, and fascinating it by sympathy, will find that he has, within moral limits, a strange power of fascinating those who are in sympathy with him.

Whereupon many will say "of course." Like and like together strike. Birds of a feather flock together. *Similis similibus.* But it often happens in this life, though they meet they do *not* pair off. Very often indeed they meet, but to part. There must be, even where the affinity exists, consideration and forethought to test the affinity. It requires long practice even for keen eyes to recognize the amethyst or topaz, or many other gems, in their natural state as sea-worn pebbles. Now, it is not a matter of fancy, of romance, or imagination, that there are men and women who really have, deeply hidden in their souls, or more objectively manifested, peculiar or beautiful characteristics, or a spirit. I would not speak here merely of *naïveté* or tenderness—a natural affinity for poetry, art, or beauty, but the peculiar tone and manner of it, which is sympathetic to ours. For two people may love music, yet be widely removed from all agreement if one be a Wagnerian, and the other of an older school. Suffice it to say that such similarities of mind or mood, of intellect or emotion do exist, and when they are real, and not imaginary, or merely the result of passional attraction, they suggest and may well attract the use of Fascination.

Those who actually develop within themselves such a spirit, regarding it as one, that is a self beyond self, attain to a power which few understand, which is practical, positive, and real, and not at all a superstitious fancy. It may begin in imagining or fancy, but as the veriest dream is material and may be repeated till we see it visibly and can then copy it, so can we create in ourselves a being, a segregation of our noblest thoughts, a superb abstraction of soul which looks from its sunny mountain height down on the dark and noisome valley which forms our worldly common intellect or mind, or the only one known to by far the majority of mankind, albeit they may have therein glimpses of light and truth. But it is to him who makes for himself, by earnest Will and Thought, a *separate* and better Life or Self that a better life is given.

Those who possess genius or peculiarly cultivated minds of a highly moral caste, gifted with pure integrity, and above vulgarity and worldly commonplace habits, should never form a tie in friendship or love without much forethought. And then if the active agent has disciplined his mind by self-hypnotism until he can control or manage his Will with ease, he will know without further instruction how to fascinate, and that properly and legitimately.

Those who now acquire this power are few and far between, and when they *really* possess it they make no boast nor parade, but rather keep it carefully to themselves, perfectly content with what it yields for reward. And here I may declare something in which I firmly believe, yet which very few I fear will understand as I mean it. If this fascination and other faculties like it may be called Magical (albeit all is within the limits of science and matter), then there are assuredly in this world magicians whom we meet without dreaming that they are such. Here and there, however rare, there is mortal who has studied deeply—but

> "Softened all and tempered into beauty;
> And blended with lone thoughts and wanderings,
> The quest of hidden knowledge, and a mind
> To *love* the universe."

Such beings do not come before the world, but hide their lights, knowing well that their magic would defeat itself, and perish if it were made common. Any person of the average worldly cast who could work any miracles, however small, would in the end bitterly regret it if he allowed it to be known. Thus I have read ingenious stories, as for instance one by HOOD, showing what terrible troubles a man fell into by being able to make himself invisible. Also another setting forth the miseries of a successful alchemist. The Algonkin Indians have a legend of a man who came to grief and death through his power of making all girls love him. But the magic of which I speak is of a far more subtle and deeply refined nature, and those who possess it are alone in life, save when by some rare chance they meet their kind. Those who are deeply and mysteriously interested in any pursuit for which the great multitude of all-alike people have no sympathy, who have peculiar studies and subjects of thought, partake a little of the nature of the *magus*. Magic, as popularly understood, has no existence, it is a literal *myth*—for it means nothing but what amazes or amuses for a short time. No miracle would be one if it became common. Nature is infinite, therefore its laws cannot be violated— *ergo,* there is no magic if we mean by that an inexplicable contravention of law.

But that there are minds who have simply advanced in knowledge beyond the multitude in certain things which cannot at once be made common property is true, for there is a great deal of marvelous truth not as yet dreamed of even by HERBERT SPENCERS or EDISONS, by RONTGENS or other scientists. And yet herein is hidden the greatest secret of future human happenings.

> "What I was is passed by,
> What I am away doth fly;
> What I shall be none do see,
> Yet in that my glories be."

Now to illustrate this more clearly. Some of these persons who are more or less secretly addicted to magic (I say secretly, because they cannot make it known if they would), take the direction of feeling or living with inexpressible enjoyment in the beauties of nature. That, they attain to something almost or quite equal to life in Fairyland, is conclusively proved by the fact that only very rarely, here and there in their best passages, do the greatest poets more than imperfectly and briefly convey some broken idea or reflection of the feelings which are excited by thousands of subjects in nature in many. The Mariana of TENNYSON surpasses anything known to me in any language as conveying the reality of feeling alone in a silent old house, where everything is a dim, uncanny manner, recalled the past—yet suggested a kind of mysterious presence—as in the passage:

> "All day within the dreary house
> The doors upon their hinges creaked,
> The blue fly sang in the pane, the mouse
> Behind the mouldering wainscot shrieked,
> Or from the crevice peered about;

Old faces glimmered thro' the doors,
Old footsteps trod the upper floors,
Old voices called her from without."

Yet even this unsurpassed poem does no more than *partially* revive and recall the reality to me of similar memories of long, long ago, when an invalid child I was often left in a house entirely alone, from which even the servants had absented themselves. Then I can remember how after reading the Arabian Nights or some such unearthly romance, as was the mode in the Thirties, the very sunshine stealing craftily and silently like a living thing, in a bar through the shutter, twinkling with dust, as with infinitely small stars, living and dying like sparks, the buzzing of the flies who were little blue imps, with now and then a larger Beelzebub—a strange imagined voice ever about, which seemed to *say* something without words—and the very furniture, wherein the chairs were as goblins, and the broom a tall young woman, and the looking-glass a kind of other self-life—all of this as I recall it appears to me as a picture of the absence of human beings as described by TENNYSON, *plus* a strange personality in every object—which the poet does not attempt to convey. This is, however, a very small or inferior illustration; there are far more remarkable and deeply spiritual or æsthetically-suggestive subjects than this, and that in abundance, which Art has indeed so reproduced as to amaze the many who have only had snatches of such observation themselves.

But the magicians, SHELLEY, or KEATS, or WORDSWORTH, only convey *partial* echoes of certain subjects, or of their specialties. It is indeed beautiful to feel what Art can do, but the original is worth far more. And if the reader would be such a magician, let him give his heart and will to taking an interest in all that is beautiful, good and true—or honest. For that it really can be done in all fullness is true beyond a dream of doubt. By the ordinary methods of learning one may indeed acquire an exact, mechanically drawn picture, which we modify with what beauty chance bestows. But he who will learn by the process which I have endeavored to describe, or by studying with the *will*, cannot fail to experience a strange enchantment in so doing, as I have read in an Italian tale of a youth who was sadly weary of his lessons, but who, being taken daily by certain kind fairies into their school on a hill, found all difficulties disappear and the pursuit of knowledge as joyful as that of pleasure.

I have heard hypnotism, with regard to fascination, spoken of with great apprehension. "It is dreadful," said one to me, "to think of anybody's being able to exercise such an influence on anyone." And yet, widely known as it is, instances of its abuse are very rare. Thus, when Cremation was first discussed, it was warmly opposed, because somebody *might* be poisoned, and then, the body being burned, there could be no autopsy! Nature has decreed some drawback to the best things; nothing is perfect. But to balance the immense benefits latent in suggestion against the problematic abuses is like condemning the ship because a bucket of tar has been spilt on the deck.

Sincere kindness and respect, which are allied unto identity, are the best or surest key to love, and they in turn are allied to fascination. Here I might observe that the action of the eye, which is a silent speech of emotion, has always been regarded as powerful in fascination, but those who are not by nature gifted with it cannot use it to much good purpose. That emotional, susceptible subjects ready to receive suggestion can be put to sleep or made to imagine anything terrible regarding anybody's glance is very true, just as an ignorant Italian will believe of any man that he has the *malocchio* if he be told so, whence came the idea that Pope Gregory XVI had the evil eye. But where there is *sincere* kindly feeling it makes itself felt in a sympathetic nature by what is popularly called magic, only because it is not understood. The enchantment lies in this, that unconscious cerebration, or the power (or powers), who are always acting in us, effect many curious and very subtle mental phenomena, all of which they do not confide to the common-sense waking judgment or Reason, simply because the latter is almost entirely occupied with common worldly subjects. It is as if someone whose whole attention and interest had been at all times given to some plain hard drudgery, should be called on to review or write a book of exquisitely subtle poetry. It is, indeed, almost sadly touching to reflect how this innocent and beautiful faculty of recognizing what is good, is really acting perhaps in evil and merely worldly minds all in vain, and all unknown to them. The more the conscious waking-judgment has been trained to recognize goodness, the more will the hidden water-fairies rise above the surface, as it were, to the sunshine. So it comes that true kindly feeling is recognized by sympathy, and those who would be loved, cannot do better than make themselves truly and perfectly *kind* by forethought and will, and with this the process of self-hypnotism will be a great aid. For it is not more by winning others to us, than in willing ourselves to them that true Love consists.

Love or trusting sympathy from any human being, however humble, is the most charming thing in life, and it ought to be the main object of existence. Yet there are thousands all round us, yes, many among our friends or acquaintances, who live and die without ever having known it, because in their egotism and folly they conceive of close relations as founded on personal power, interest or the weakness of others. The only fascination which such people can ever exercise is that of the low and devilish kind, the influence of the cat on the mouse, the eye of the snake on the bird, which in the end degrades them into deeper evil. That there are such people, and that they really make captive and oppress weaker minds, by suggestion, is true; the marvel being that so few find it out.

But in proportion as this kind of fascination is vile and mean, that which may be called altruistic or sympathetic attraction, or Enchantment, is noble and pure, because it acquires strength in proportion to the purity and beauty of the soul or will which inspires it. It is as real and has as much power, and can be exercised by any honest person whatever with wonderful effect, even to the performing what are popularly called "miracles," which only means wonderful works beyond *our* power of explanation. But this kind of fascination is little understood as yet, simply because it is based on purity, morality and light, and hitherto the seekers for occult mysteries have been chiefly occupied with the gloomy and mock-diabolical rubbish of old tradition, instead of scientific investigation of our minds and brains.

There is also in truth a Fascination by means of the Voice, which has in it a much deeper and stronger power or action than that of merely sweet sound as of an instrument. The Jesuit, GASPAR SCHOTT, in his *Magio Medica* treats of Fascination as twofold: *De Fascinatione per Visunt et Vocem*. I have found among Italian witches as with Red Indian wizards, every magical operation depended on an incantation, and every incantation on the feeling, intonation, or manner in which it is sung. Thus near Rome any peasant overhearing a *scongiurasione* would recognize it from the *sound* alone.

Anyone, male or female, can have a deep, rich voice by simply subduing and training it, and very rarely raising it to a high pitch. *Nota bene* that the less this is affected the more effective it will be. There are many, especially women, who speak, as it were, all time in italics, when they do not set their speech in small caps or displayed large capitals. The result of this, as regards sound, is the so-called nasal voice, which is very much like caterwauling, and I need not say that there is no fascination in it—on the contrary its tendency is to destroy any other kind of attraction. It is generally far more due to an ill-trained, unregulated, excitable, nervous temperament than to any other cause.

The training the voice to a subdued state "like music in its softest key," or to rich, deep tones, though it be done artificially, has an extraordinary effect on the character and on others. It is associated with a well-trained mind and one gifted with self-control. One of the richest voices to which I ever listened was that of the poet TENNYSON. I can remember another man of marvelous mind, vast learning, and æsthetic-poetic power who also had one of those voices which exercised great influence on all who heard it.

There is an amusing parallel as regards nasal-screaming voices in the fact that a donkey cannot bray unless he at the same time lifts his tail—but if the tail be *tied down,* the beast must be silent. So the man or woman, whose voice like that of the erl-king's is "ghostly shrill as the wind in the porch of a ruined church," always raise their tones with their temper, but if we keep the former down by training, the latter cannot rise.

I once asked a very talented lady teacher of Elocution in Philadelphia if she regarded shrill voices as incurable. She replied that they invariably yielded to instruction and training. Children under no domestic restraint who were allowed to scream out and dispute on all occasions and were never corrected in intonation, generally had vulgar voices.

A good voice acts very evidently on the latent powers of the mind, and impresses the æsthetic sense, even when it is unheeded by the conscious judgment. Many a clergyman makes a deep impression by his voice alone.

And why? Certainly not by appealing to the reason. Therefore it is well to be able to fascinate with the voice. Now, *nota bene*—as almost every human being can speak in a soft or well-toned voice, "at least, subdued unto a temperate tone" just as long as he or she chooses to do it, it follows that with foresight, aided by suggestion, or continued will, we can all acquire this enviable accomplishment.

To end this chapter with a curious bit of appropriate folk-lore, I would record that while Saxo Grammaticus, Olaus Magnus, and a host of other Norsemen have left legends to prove that there were sorcerers who by magic of the soft and wondrous voice could charm and capture men of the sword, so the Jesuit ATHANASIUS KIRCHER, declares that on the seventeenth day of May, 1638, he, going from Messina in a boat, witnessed with his own eyes the capture not of swordsmen but of sundry *xiphiæ*, or sword-fish, by means of a melodiously chanted charm, the words whereof he noted down as follows:

"Mammassudi di pajanu,
Palletu di pajanu,
Majassu stigneta.
Pallettu di pajanu,
Palè la stagneta.
Mancata stigneta.
Pro nastu varitu pressu du
Visu, e da terra!"

Of which words Kircher declares that they are probably of mingled corrupt Greek and ancient Sicilian, but that whatever they are, they certainly are admirable for the catching of fish.

CHAPTER X.

THE SUBLIMINAL SELF.

While the previous pages of this work were in the press, I received and read a very interesting and able Book, entitled, "Telepathy and the Subliminal

Self, or an account of recent investigations regarding Hypnotism, Automatism, Dreams, Phantoms, and related phenomena," by R. OSGOOD MASON, A.M., Fellow of the New York Academy of Medicine. Dr. MASON, on the whole, may be said to follow HARTMANN, since he places Thaumaturgy, or working what have been considered as wonders, miracles, and the deeds of spiritualists, on the evolutionary or material basis. He is also far less superstitious or prone to seek the miraculous and mysterious for its own sake, than his predecessors in *occulta*, and limits his beliefs to proofs sustained by good authority. He recognizes a second, or what he calls a subliminal Self, the Spirit of our Soul, acting independently of Waking Conscious Judgment, a mysterious *alter ego*, which has marvelous power.

This second or inner self I have also through this work of mine recognized as a reality, though it is, like the self-conscious soul, rather an aggregate than a distinct unity. Thus we may for convenience sake speak of the Memory, when there are in fact millions of memories, since every image stored away in the brain is one, and the faculty of revising them for the use of the waking soul, is certainly apart from the action of bringing them into play in dreams. In fact if we regard the action of all known faculties, we might assume with the Egyptians that man had not merely eight distinct souls, but eighty, or even a countless number. And as the ancients, knowing very little about mental action, classed it all as one soul, so we may call that which is partially investigated and mysterious, a second or inner "soul," spirit, or subliminal self—that is to say provisionally, till more familiar with its nature and relations.

DR. MASON, to his credit be it said, has not accepted for Gospel, as certain French writers have done, the tricks of self-confessed humbugs. He has only given us the cream of the most strictly attested cases, as related by French scientists and people of unquestioned veracity. And yet admitting that in every instance the witness sincerely believed that he or she spoke the truth, the aggregate is so far from confirming the tales told, that consideration and comparison would induce very grave doubt. Thus, who could have been more sincere, purely honest or pious than JUSTINUS KERNER, whom I knew personally, SWEDENBORG, ESCHENMAYER and all of their school? Yet how utterly irreconcilable are all their revelations!

Therefore, while I have cited illustration and example as affording unproved or hearsay evidence, I, in fact, decidedly reject not only all tradition, as proof on occult subjects, but all assertion from any quarter, however trustworthy, asking the reader to believe in nothing which he cannot execute and make sure unto himself. Tradition and testimony are very useful to supply ideas or theories, but to actually *believe* in anything beyond his experience a man should take sufficient interest in it to *prove* it by personal experiment. And, therefore, as I have already declared, I not only ask, but hope that no reader will put faith in anything which I have alleged or declared, until he has fully and fairly proved it to be true in his own person.

The history of true culture, truth, or progress has been that of doubt or disbelief in all which cannot be scientifically proved or made manifest to sensation and reflection, and even in this the most scrupulous care must be exercised, since our senses often deceive us. Therefore, in dealing with subjects which have undeniably been made the means of deceit and delusion thousands of times to one authentic instance, it is not well to accept testimony, or any kind of evidence, or proof, save that which we can establish for ourself. The day is not yet, but it is coming, when self-evidence will be claimed, and granted, as to all human knowledge, and the sooner it comes the better will it be for the world.

But I would be clearly understood as declaring that it is only as regards making up our minds to absolute faith in what involves what may be called our mental welfare, which includes the most serious conduct of life, that I would limit belief to scientific proof. As an example, I will cite the very interesting case of the hypnotic treatment of a patient by DR. VOISIN, and as given by MASON.

"In the summer of 1884, there was at the Salpêtrière a young woman of a deplorable type, Jeanne S—, who was a criminal lunatic, filthy, violent, and with a life history of impurity and crime. M. Auguste Voisin, one of the physicians of the staff, undertook to hypnotize her, May 31. At that time she was so violent that she could only be kept quiet by a straight-jacket and the constant cold douche to her head. She would not look at M. Voisin, but raved and spat at him. He persisted, kept his face near and opposite to hers, and his eyes following hers constantly. In ten minutes she was in a sound sleep, and soon passed into a somnambulistic condition. The process was repeated many days, and she gradually became sane while in the hypnotic condition, but still raved when she woke.

"Gradually then she began to accept hypnotic suggestion, and would obey trivial orders given her while asleep, such as to sweep her room, then suggestions regarding her general behavior; then, in her hypnotic condition, she began to express regret for her past life, and form resolutions of amendment to which she finally adhered when she awoke. Two years later she was a nurse in one of the Paris hospitals, and her conduct was irreproachable. M. Voisin has followed up this case by others equally striking."

This is not only an unusually well authenticated instance, but one which seems to carry conviction from the manner of narration. Yet it would be absurd to declare that the subject neither deceived herself nor others, or that the doctor made no mistakes either in fact or involuntarily. The whole is, however, extremely valuable from its *probability*, and still more from its suggesting experiment in a much more useful direction than that followed in the majority of cases recorded in most books, which, especially in France, seem chiefly to have been conducted from a melodramatic or merely medical point of view. Very few indeed seem to have ever dreamed that a hypnotized subject was anything but a being to be cured of some disorder, operated on without pain, or made to undergo and perform various tricks, often extremely cruel, silly, and wicked—the main object of all being to advertise the skill of the operator. In fact, if it were to be accepted that the main object of hypnotism is to repeat such experiments as are described in most of the French works on the subject, humanity and decency would join in prohibiting the practice of the art altogether. These books point out and make clear in the minutest manner, how every kind of crime can be committed, and the mind brought to regard all that is evil as a matter of course. The making an innocent person attempt to commit a murder or steal is among the most usual experiments; while, on the contrary, any case like that of the reform of Jeanne S— is either very rare, or else is treated simply as a proof of the skill of some *medico*. The fact that if the successes which are recorded are *true,* there exists a *stupendous* power by means of which the average morality and happiness of mankind can be incredibly advanced and sustained, and Education, Art in every branch, and, in a word, all Culture be marvelously developed on a far more secure basis than in the old systems, does not seem to have occurred to any of those who possessed, as it were, gold, without having the least idea of its value or even its qualities.

Happiness in the main is a pleasant, contented condition of the mind, that is to say, "a state of mind." To be perfect, as appears from an enlarged study of all things or phenomena in their relations (since every part must harmonize with the whole), this happiness implies duty and altruism, every whit as much as self-enjoyment. This agrees with and results from scientific experience. Under the old *a priori* psychologic system, *selfishness* (which meant that every soul was to be chiefly or solely concerned in saving itself, guided by hope of reward and fear of punishment), it was naturally the basis of morality.

Now, accepting the definition of Happiness as a state of mind under certain conditions, it follows that it can be realized to a great degree, and in all cases to some degree, firstly by forethought or carefully defining what it is or what we desire, and secondly by making a fixed idea by simple, well-nigh mechanical means, without any resource to *les grands môyens*. According to the old and now rapidly vanishing philosophy, this was to be effected by sublime morality, prayer, or adjuration of supernatural beings and noble heroism, but what is here proposed is much humbler, albeit more practical. Reading immortal poetry or prose is indeed a splendid power, but to learn the letters of the alphabet, and to spell, is very simple and unpoetic, yet far more practical. What I have described has been the mere dull rudiments. It is most remarkable that the world has always known that the art of RAFFAELLE, MICHAEL ANGELO, and ALBERT DURER was based, like that of the greatest musicians, on extensive rudimentary study, and yet has never dreamed that what far surpasses all art in every way, and even includes the desire for it, may all proceed from, or be developed by, a process which is even easier than those required for the lesser branches.

He who can control his own mind by an iron will, and say to the Thoughts which he would banish, "Be ye my slaves and begone into outer darkness," or to Peace "Dwell with me forever, come what may," *and be obeyed*, that man is a mighty magician who has attained what is worth more than all that Earth possesses. Absolute self-control under the conditions before defined—since our happiness to be true must agree with that of others—is absolutely essential to happiness. There can be no greater hero than the man who can conquer himself and think exactly as he pleases. That which annoys, tempts, stirs us to being irritable, wicked, or mean, is an aggregate of evil thoughts or images received by chance or otherwise into the memory, developed there into vile unions, and new forms like coalescing animalcule, and so powerful and vivid or objective do they become that men in all ages have given them a real existence as evil spirits.

Every sane man living, can if he *really* desires it, obtain complete absolute command of himself, exorcise these vile demons and bring in peace instead, by developing with determination the simple process which I have described. I have found in my own experience a fierce pleasure in considering obnoxious and pernicious Thoughts as imps or demons to be conquered, in which case Pride and even Arrogance become virtues, even as poisons in their place are wholesome medicines. Thus, he who is haunted with the fixed idea, even well nigh to monomania, that he will never give way to ill temper, that nothing shall disturb his equanimity, need not fear evil results any more than the being haunted by angels. Now we can all have fixed or haunting ideas, on any subject which we please to entertain—but the idea to create good and beneficent haunting has not, that I am aware, been suggested by philosophers.

That mental influence can be exerted hypnotically most directly and certainly by one person upon another is undeniable, but this requires, firstly, a susceptible subject, or only one person in three or four, and to a degree a specially gifted operator, and very often "heaven-sent moments."

"However greatly mortals may require it,
All cannot go to Corinth who desire it."

But forethought, self-suggestion, and the bringing the mind to dwell continuously on a subject are absolutely within the reach of all who have any strength of mind whatever, without any aid. Those of feebler ability yield, however, all the more readily (as in the case of children) to the influence of others or of hypnotism by a master. Therefore, either subjectively or with assistance, most human beings can be morally benefited to a limitless degree, "morally" including intellectually.

We often hear it said of a person that he or she would do well or succeed if that individual had "application." Now, as Application, or "sticking to it," or perseverance in earnest faith, is the main condition for success in all that I have discussed, I trust that it will be borne in mind that the process indicated provides from the first lesson or experiment for this chief requisite. For the *fore-thinking* and hypnotizing our minds to be in a certain state or condition all the next day, by what some writers, such as HARTMANN, treat as magical process—but which is just so much magical as the use of an electrical machine—is simply a beginning in Attention and Perseverance.

> "So, like a snowball rolled in falling snow,
> It gathers size as it doth onward go."

When we make a wish or will, or determine that in future after awaking we shall be in a given state of mind, we also include Perseverance for the given time, and as success supposes repetition in all minds, it follows that Perseverance will be induced gradually and easily.

And here I may remark that while all writers on ethics, duty or morals, cry continually "Be persevering, be honest, be enterprising, exert your will!" and so on, and waste thousands of books in illustrating the advantages of all these fine things, there is not one who tells us *how* to practically execute or do them. To follow the hint of a quaint Sunday School picture, they show us a swarm of Bees, with hive and honey, but do not tell us how to catch *one*. And yet a man may be anything he pleases if he will by easy and simple practice as I have shown, make the conception habitual. I do not tell you as these good folk do, how to go about it nobly, or heroically, or piously; in fact, I prescribe a method as humble as making a fire, or a pair of shoes, and yet in very truth and honor I have profited far more by it than I ever did from all the exhortations which I ever have read.

Now there are many men who are not so bad in themselves in reality, but who are so haunted by evil thoughts, impulses, and desires, that they, being taught by the absurd old heathenish psychology that the "soul" is all one spiritual entity, believe themselves to be as wicked as Beelzebub could wish, when, in fact, these sins are nothing but evil weeds which came into the mind as neglected seeds, and grew apace from sheer carelessness. Regarding them in the light, as one may say, of bodily and material nuisances, or a kind of vermin, they can be extirpated by the strong hand of Will, much more easily than under the old system, whereby they were treated with respect and awe as MILTON hath done (and most immorally too), DANTE being no better; and they would both have exerted their gigantic intellects to better purpose by showing man how to conquer the devil, instead of exalting and exaggerating his stupendous power and showing how, as regards Humanity (for which expressly the Universe, including countless millions of solar systems, was created), Satan has by far the victory, since he secures the majority of souls. For saying which thing a holy bishop once got himself into no end of trouble.

I say that he who uses his will can crush and drive out vile haunting thoughts, and the more rudely and harshly he does it the better. In all the old systems, without exception, they are treated with far too much respect and reverence, and no great wonder either, since they were regarded as a great innate portion of the soul. Whether to be cleared out by the allopathic exorcism, or the gentler homœpathic prayer, the patient never relied on himself. There is a fine Italian proverb in the collection of GUILLO VARRINO, Venice 1656, which declares that *Buona volontà supplice à facolta*—"strong will ekes out ability"—and before the Will (which the Church has ever weakened or crushed) no evil instincts can hold. The same author tells us that "The greatest man in the world is he who can govern his own will," also, "To him who wills naught is impossible." To which I would add that "Whoever chooses to have a will may do so by culture," or by ever so little to begin with. Nay, I have no doubt that in time there will be societies, schools, churches, or circles, in which the Will shall be taught and applied to all moral and mental culture.

He who wills it sincerely can govern his Will, and he who can govern his Will is a thousand times more fortunate than if he could govern the world.

For to govern the Will is to be without fear, superior and indifferent to all earthly follies and shams, idols, cants and delusions, it is to be lord of a thousand isles in the sea of life, and absolutely greater than any living mortal, as men exist. Small need has that man to heed what his birth or station in society may be who has mastered himself with the iron will; for he who has conquered death and the devil need fear no shadows.

He who masters himself by Will has attained to all that is best and noblest in Stoicism, Epicureanism, Christianity, and Agnosticism; if the latter be understood not as doubt, but free Inquiry, and could men be made to feel what all this means and what power it bestows, and how easily it really is to master it, we should forthwith see all humanity engaged in the work.

It has been declared by many in the past in regard to schooling their minds to moral and practical ends that, leading busy lives, they had not time to think of such matters. But I earnestly protest that it is these very men of all others who most require the discipline which I have taught, and it is as easy for them as for anybody; as it, indeed, ought to be easier, yes, and far more profitable. For the one who leads by fortune a quiet life of leisure can often school himself without a system, while he who toils amid anxious thoughts and with every mental power severely taxed, will find that he can do his work *far* more easily if he determines that he *will* master it. The amount of mental action which lies dormant in us all is illimitable and it can all be realized by the hypnotism of Will.

CHAPTER XI.

PARACELSUS.

That our ordinary consciousness or Waking Intellect, and what is generally recognized as Mind or Soul, includes whatever has been taken in by sensation and reflection and assimilated to daily wants, or shows itself in bad or good memories and thought, is evident. Not less clear is it that there is another hidden Self—a power which, recognizing much which is evil in the Mind, would fain reject, or rule, or subdue it. This latent, inner Intelligence calls into action the Will. All of this is vague, and, it may be, unscientific. It is more rational to believe in many faculties or functions, but the classification here suggested may serve as a basis. It is effectively that of GRASSNER, or of all who have recognized the power of the Will to work "miracles," guided by a higher morality. And it is very curious that PARACELSUS based his whole system of nervous cure, at least, on this theory. Thus, in the *Liber Entium Morborum, de Ente Spirituali,* chap, iii, he writes:

"As we have shown that there are two *Subjecta*, this will we assume as our ground. Ye know that there is in the Body a Soul. *(Geist.)* Now reflect, to what purpose? Just that it may sustain life, even as the air keeps animals from dying for want of breath. So we know what the soul is. This soul in Man is actually clear, intelligible and sensible to the other soul, and, classing them, they are to be regarded as allied, even as bodies are. I have a soul—the *other* hath also one."

PARACELSUS is here very obscure, but he manifestly means by "the other," the Body. To resume:

"The Souls know one another as 'I,' and 'the other.' They converse together in their language, not by necessity according to our thoughts, but what *they* will. And note, too, that there may be anger between them, and one may belittle or injure the other; this injury is in the Soul, the Soul in the body. Then the body suffers and is ill—not materially or from a material *Ens*, but from the Soul. For this we need spiritual remedy. Ye are two who are dear unto one another; great in affinity. The cause is not *in* the body, nor is it from without; it comes from your souls *(Geisten)*, who are allied. The same pair may become inimical, or remain so. And that ye may understand a cause for this, note that the Spirit *(Geist)* of the Reasoning Faculty *(Vernunft)* is not born, save from the *Will*, therefore the Will and the Reason are separate. What exists and acts according to the Will lives in the Spirit; what only according to the Reason lives against the Spirit. For the Reason brings forth no spirit, only the Soul *(Seel)* is born of it—from Will comes the Spirit, the essence of which we describe and let the Soul be."

In this grandly conceived but most carelessly written passage the author, in the beginning thereof, makes such confusion in expressing both Soul and Spirit with the one word, *Geist,* that his real meaning could not be intelligible to the reader who had not already mastered the theory. But, in fact, the whole conception is marvelous, and closely agreeing with the latest discoveries in Science, while ignoring all the old psychological system.

Very significant is what PARACELSUS declares in his *Fragmenta Medicina de Morbis Somnii*, that so many evils beset us, "caused by the coarseness of our ignorance, because we know not what is born in us." That is to say, if we knew our mental power, or what we are capable of, we could cure or control all bodily infirmities. And how to rule and form this power, and make it obey the *Geist* or Will which PARACELSUS believed was born of the common conscious Soul—that is the question.

For PARACELSUS truly believed that out of this common Soul, the result of Sensation and Reflection, and all we pick up by Experience and Observation (and such as makes all that there is of Life for most people), there is born, or results, a perception of Ideas, of right and wrong, of mutual interests; a certain subtle, moral conscience or higher knowledge. "The Souls may become inimical;" that is, the Conscience, or Spirit, may differ or disagree with the Soul, as a son may be at variance with his father. So the flower or fruit may oft despise the root. The Will is allied to Conscience or a perception of the Ideal. When a man finds out that he knows more or better than he has hitherto done: as, for instance, when a thief learns that it is wrong to steal, and feels it deeply, he endeavors to reform, although he *feels* all the time old desires and temptations to rob. Now, if he resolutely subdue these, his Will is born. "The spirit of the Reasoning faculty is not born, save of the Will. . . . what exists and acts according to the Will lives in the spirit." The perception of ideals is the bud, Conscience the flower, and the Will the fruit. A pure Will must be *moral*, for it is *the* result of the perception of Ideals, or a Conscience. The world in general regards Will as mere blind force, applicable to good or bad indifferently. But the more truly and fully it is developed, or as Orson is raised to Valentine, the more moral and optimistic does it become. *Will* in its perfection is Genius, spontaneous originality, that is Voluntary; not merely a power to lift a weight, or push a load, or force others to yield, but the Thought itself which suggests the deed and finds a *reason* for it. Now the merely unscrupulous use of Opportunity and Advantage, or Crime, is popularly regarded as having a strong Will; but this, as compared to a Will with a conscience, is as the craft of the fox compared to that of the dragon, and that of the dragon to Siegfried.

And here it may be observed as a subtle and strange thing, approaching to magic apparently, as understood by HARTMANN and his school, that the Will sometimes, when much developed, actually manifests something like an independent personality, or at least seems to do so, to an acute observer. And what is more remarkable, it can have this freedom of action and invention delegated to it, and will act on it.

Thus, in conversation with HERKOMER, the Artist, and Dr. W. W. BALDWIN, Nov. 2d, 1878, the former explained to me that when he would execute a work of art, he just determined it with care or Forethought in his mind, and gave it a rest, as by sleep, during which time it unconsciously fructified or germinated, even as a seed when planted in the ground at last grows upward into the light and air. Now, that the entire work should not be too much finished or quite completed, and to leave room for after-thoughts or possible improvements, he was wont, as he said, to give the Will some leeway, or freedom; which is the same thing as if, before going to sleep, we *Will* or determine that on the following day our Imagination, or Creative Force, or Inventive Genius, shall be unusually active, which will come to pass after some small practice and a few repetitions, as all may find for themselves. Truly, it will be according to conditions, for if there be but little in a man, either he will bring but little out, or else he must wait until he can increase what he hath. And in this the Will *seems* to act like an independent person, ingeniously, yet withal obedient. And the same also characterizes images in dreams, which sometimes appear to be so real that it is no wonder many think they are spirits from another world, as is true of many haunting thoughts which come unbidden. However, this is all mere Thaumaturgy, which has been so deadly to Truth in the old *à priori* psychology, and still works mischief, albeit it has its value in suggesting very often in Poetry what Science afterwards proves in Prose.

To return to PARACELSUS, HEINE complains that his German is harder to understand than his Latin. However, I think that in the following passages he shows distinctly a familiarity with hypnotism, or certainly, passes by hand and suggestion. Thus, chap, x, *de Ente Spirituali*, in which the Will is described, begins as follows: "Now shall ye mark that the Spirits rule their subjects. And I have shown intelligibly how the *Ens Spirituale,* or Spiritual Being, rules so mightily the body that many disorders may be ascribed to it. Therefore unto these ye should not apply ordinary medicine, but heal the spirit—therein lies the disorder."

PARACELSUS clearly states that by the power of Foresight—he uses the exact word, *Fürsicht*—Man may, aided by Sleep, attain to knowledge—past, present or future—and achieve Telepathy, or communion at a distance. In the *Fragmenta, Caput de Morbis Somnii* he writes:

"Therefore learn, that by Foresight man can know future things; and, from experience, the past and present. Thereby is man so highly gifted in Nature that he knows or perceives *(sicht),* as he goes, his neighbor or friend in a distant land. Yet, on waking, he knows nothing of all this. For God has given to us all—Art, Wisdom, Reason—to know the future, and what passes in distant lands; but we know it not, for we fools, busied in common things, sleep away, as it were, what is in us. Thus, seeing one who is a better artist than thou art, do not say that he has more gift or grace than thou; for thou hast it also, but hast not tried, and so is it with all things. What Adam and Moses did was to *try,* and they succeeded, and it came neither from the Devil nor from Spirits, but from the Light of Nature, which they developed in themselves. But we do *not* seek for what is in us, therefore we remain nothing, and are nothing."

Here the author very obscurely, yet vigorously, declares that we can do or learn what we *will,* but it must be achieved by foresight, will, and the aid of sleep.

It seems very evident, after careful study of the text, that here, as in many other places, our author indicates familiarity with the method of developing mental action in its subtlest and most powerful forms. Firstly, by determined Foresight, and, secondly, by the aid of sleep, corresponding to the bringing a seed to rest a while, and thereby cause it to germinate; the which admirable simile he himself uses in a passage which I have not cited.

PARACELSUS was the most original thinker and the worst writer of a wondrous age, when all wrote badly and thought badly. There is in his

German writings hardly one sentence which is not ungrammatical, confused, or clumsy; nor one without a vigorous idea, which shows the mind or character of the man.

As a curious instance of the poetic originality of PARACELSUS we may take the following:

"It is an error to suppose that chiromancy is limited to the hand, for there are significant lines (indicating character), all over the body. And it is so in vegetable life. For in a plant every leaf is a hand. Man hath two; a tree many, and every one reveals its anatomy—a hand-anatomy. Now ye shall understand that in double form the lines are masculine or feminine. And there are as many differences in these lines on leaves as in human hands."

GOETHE has the credit that he reformed or advanced the Science of Botany, by reducing the plant to the leaf as the germ or type; and this is now further reduced to the cell, but the step was a great one. Did not PARACELSUS, however, give the idea?

"The theory of signatures," says VAUGHAN, in his *Hours with the Mystics*, "proceeded on the supposition that every creatures bears in some part of its structure . . . the indication of the character or virtue inherent in it—the representation, in fact, of its ideal or soul. . . . The student of sympathies thus essayed to read the character of plants by signs in their organization, as the professor of palmistry announced that of men by lines in the hand." Thus, to a degree which is very little understood, PARACELSUS took a great step towards modern science. He disclaimed Magic and Sorcery, with ceremonies, and endeavored to base all cure on human will. The name of PARACELSUS is now synonymous with Rosicrucianism, Alchemy, Elementary Spirits and Theurgy, when, in fact, he was in his time a bold reformer, who cast aside an immense amount of old superstition, and advanced into what his age regarded as terribly free thought. He was compared to LUTHER, and the doing so greatly pleased him; he dwells on it at length in one of his works.

What PARACELSUS really believed in at heart was nothing more or less than an unfathomable Nature, a *Natura naturans* of infinite resource, connected with which, as a microcosm, is man, who has also within him infinite powers, which he can learn to master by cultivating the will, which must be begun at least by the aid of sleep, or letting the resolve ripen, as it were, in the mind, apart from Consciousness.

I had written every line of my work on the same subject and principles long before I was aware that I had unconsciously followed exactly in the footprints of the great Master; for though I had made many other discoveries in his books, I knew nothing of this.

CHAPTER XII.

LAST WORDS.

"By carrying calves Milo, 'tis said, grew strong,
Until with ease he bore a bull along."

It is, I believe, unquestionable that, if he ever lived, a man who had attained to absolute control over his own mind, must have been the most enviable of mortals. MONTAIGNE illustrates such an ideal being by a quotation from VIRGIL:

"Velut rupes vastum quæ prodit in æquor
Obvia ventorum furiis, exposta que ponto,
   Vim cunctum atque minas perfert cælique marisque
Ipsa immota manens."

"He as a rock among vast billows stood,
Scorning loud winds and the wild raging flood,
   And firm remaining, all the force defies,
From the grim threatening seas and thundering skies."

And MONTAIGNE also doubted whether such self-control was possible. He remarks of it:

"Let us never attempt these Examples; we shall never come up to them. This is too much and too rude for our common souls to undergo. CATO indeed gave up the noblest Life that ever was upon this account, but it is for us meaner spirited men to fly from the storm as far as we can."

Is it? I may have thought so once, but I begin to believe that in this darkness a new strange light is beginning to show itself. The victory may be won far more easily than the rather indolent and timid Essayist ever imagined. MONTAIGNE, and many more, believed that absolute self-control is only to be obtained by iron effort, heroic and terrible exertion—a conception based on bygone History, which is all a record of battles of man against man, or man with the Devil. Now the world is beginning slowly to make an ideal of peace, and disbelieve in the Devil. Science is attempting to teach us that from any beginning, however small, great results are sure to be obtained if resolutely followed up and fully developed.

It requires thought to realize what a man gifted to some degree with culture and common sense must enjoy who can review the past without pain, and regard the present with perfect assurance that come what may he need have no fear or fluttering of the heart. Spenser has asked in "The Fate of the Butterfly":

"What more felicity can fall to creature
Than to enjoy delight with liberty?"

To which one may truly reply that all delight is fitful and uncertain unless bound or blended with the power to be indifferent to involuntary annoying emotions, and that self-command is in itself the highest mental pleasure, or one which surpasses all of any kind. He who does not overestimate the value of money or anything earthly is really richer than the millionaire. There is a foolish story told by COMBE in his Physiology of a man who had the supernatural gift of never feeling any pain, be it from cold, hunger, heat, or accident. The rain beat upon him in vain, the keenest north wind did not chill him—he was fearless and free. But this immunity was coupled with an inability to feel pleasure—his wine or ale was no more to his palate than water, and he could not feel the kiss of his child; and so we are told that he was soon desirous to become a creature subject to all physical sensations as before. But it is, as I said, a foolish tale, because it reduces all that is worth living for to being warm or enjoying taste. His mind was not affected, but that goes for nothing in such sheer sensuality. However, a man without losing his tastes or appetites may train his Will to so master Emotion as to enjoy delight with liberty, and also exclude what constitutes the majority of all suffering with man.

It is a truth that there is very often an extremely easy, simple and prosaic way to attain many an end, which has always been supposed to require stupendous efforts. In an Italian fairy tale a prince besieges a castle with an army—trumpets blowing, banners waving, and all the pomp and circumstances of war—to obtain a beautiful heroine who is meanwhile carried away by a rival who knew of a subterranean passage. Hitherto, as I have already said, men have sought for self-control only by means of heroic exertion, or by besieging the castle from without; the simple system of Forethought and Self-Suggestion enables one, as it were, to steal or slip away with ease by night and in darkness that fairest of princesses, La Volonté, or the Will.

For he who wills to be equable and indifferent to the small and involuntary annoyances, teasing memories, irritating trifles, which constitute the chief trouble in life to most folk, can bring it about, in small measure at first and in due time to greater perfection. And by perseverance this rivulet may to a river run, the river fall into a mighty lake, and this in time rush to the roaring sea; that is to say, from bearing with indifference or quite evading attacks of *ennui,* we may come to enduring great afflictions with little suffering.

Note that I do not say that we can come to bearing all the bereavements, losses, and trials of life with *absolute* indifference. Herein MONTAIGNE and the Stoics of old were well nigh foolish to imagine such an impossible and indeed undesirable ideal. But it may be that two men are afflicted by the same domestic loss, and one with a weak nature is well nigh crushed by it, gives himself up to endless weeping and perhaps never recovers from it, while another with quite as deep feelings, but far wiser, rallies, and by vigorous exertion makes the grief a stimulus to exertion, so that while the former is demoralized, the latter is strengthened. There is an habitual state of mind by which a man while knowing his losses fully can endure them better than others, and this endurance will be greatest in him who has already cultivated it assiduously in minor matters. He who has swam in the river can swim in the sea; he who can hear a door bang without starting can listen to a cannon without jumping.

The method which I have described in this book will enable any person gifted with perseverance to make an equable or calm state of mind habitual, moderately at first, more so by practice. And when this is attained the experimenter can progress rapidly in the path. It is precisely the same as in learning a minor art, the pupil who can design a pattern (which corresponds to Foresight or plan), only requires, as in wood-carving or repoussé, to be trained by very easy process to become familiar with the use and feel of the tools, after which all that remains to be done is to keep on at what the pupil can do without the least difficulty. Well begun and well run in the end will be well done.

But glorious and marvelous is the power of him who has habituated himself by easy exercise of Will to brush away the minor, meaningless and petty cares of life, such as, however, prey on most of us; for unto him great griefs are no harder to endure than the getting a coat splashed is to an ordinary man.

www.ingramcontent.com/pod-product-compliance
Lightning Source LLC
Chambersburg PA
CBHW081122080526
44587CB00021B/3714